Entertaining
the Finnish Way
-a Feast for the Eye

Entertaining the Finnish Way is also available
in Finnish, Kotoinen pitopöytä
in Swedish, Mathälsningar från Finland
in German, Schlemmen auf Finnisch
in Norwegian, Vakre bord med god selskapsmat fra Finland
in Flemish, Feestrecepten uit Finland

Fifth edition

Editors
Helena Ahti
Leena Heikkinen
Viola Järvinen
Marjatta Pauloff

Translator
John Derome

Consultant
Raija-Leena Nyborg

Photography
Gero Mylius, photographer
Tarja Kupila, planner
Greta Baltscheffskij
Viola Järvinen
Marjatta Pauloff

Layout
Kirsi Lahti

ISBN 951-0-11293-3

Printed in WSOY Porvoo
Finland 1989

Entertaining
the Finnish Way
-a Feast for the Eye

Entertaining the Finnish Way — a Feast for the Eye

is both a modern cookbook and a guide to beautiful table setting, springing from old Finnish traditions and customs. It serves those who arrange family celebrations and wish to entertain friends and family in the vein of old traditions, but in a modern way at the same time.

Several of the old everyday recipes can today be used on more festive occasions. The dishes are tasty and simple to pre-

pare. Many cooking and baking methods of yesterday are actually modern and extremely wholesome, nutritionists claim.

Old dishes and food traditions reflect the culture of their own period. In Finland they also manifest the limitations and variety of the four seasons.

Fish was most abundantly caught in the spring after the breaking up of the ice and in the fall, when the waters had cooled. Guests and visitors got their ample share of the fish as well. Whitefish, pike perch, bream, salmon, Baltic herring or vendace were prepared for the table either in the glow of an open fire or on coals, or smoked or boiled. A speciality is still today fish which has been cured fresh with salt, pepper and dill.

This dish is known only on the shores of the clear northern waters.

At harvest time the new crop was feasted on: pea pods with melted butter, new potatoes, steamed turnip, bread baked from newly ground flour, mushrooms and berries. On cold winter days the men went hunting, and rare was the countryhouse where an elk or rabbit stew was not simmering in the oven or over the fire.

The customs and religion of our neighbors have also influenced the Finnish cuisine. The habit of eating pea soup enriched with pork, or pigs' feet, comes from East Finland's orthodox areas. It was a precaution for the beginning Lent.

In Karelia, the oven was

Table of Contents

heated daily, and pastries of various kinds and unleavened bread were eaten regardless of the occasion. In western Finland bread was baked less often but in larger batches. The loaves with a hole in the center were stored on beams in the kitchen or grain bin ceiling. Milk was made into stringy sour milk by souring it with a starter, or preserved by making it into soft and juicy cheese, according to old family recipes. Goat milk cheese from southwestern Finland is considered a fine delicacy even today. Meat and fish were preserved by smoking, to be served with sweetened potato or rutabaga dishes.

One of the best known delicacies from Lapland is reindeer. The reindeer meat in olden times was dried on the rooftops, as it still is today. Prepared in this manner it kept well and was always ready for the reindeer herdsman to take along both in summer and winter. Another excellent way to preserve the reindeer meat was to freeze it out of doors during the frost. The frozen meat was then placed in the herdsman's knapsack when he would leave to tend his herd high up on the tundra. When hunger approached, he would build a campfire and place a black kettle on it, and from the still frozen reindeer meat, he would »shave» off slivers of meat with his knife for frying. Since the development of the technique of frozen foods, it is now possible to enjoy this delicacy even in foreign countries.

The recipes in the book have been collected from this traditional material. Some of the dishes have been prepared in the original version, others have been applied to modern taste. The ingredients are simple and natural, and bring the best result without too much seasoning. The dishes are easy to prepare. The recipes are measured for ten persons, but can of course be divided, doubled or tripled according to need.

The tableware used in the photographs represent the most modern Finnish design at its best — simple and elegant. Even the cooking dishes, pots and pans can be taken directly from the oven or fire to the table, and the feasting can start!

Midsummer

It is traditional in Finland, the weather permitting, to eat out of doors on Midsummer Eve. Fresh fish, new potatoes and dill and for a delicious dessert, rhubarb pudding straight from the garden. Smoked ham and summer salad make an excellent late-night supper. The children decorate the table with birch branches and flower garlands. The potato dish sits in a garland of flowers and the table is crowned with a flower-decked, wooden tree usually used for hanging apples and candies on special occasions.

Summer lunch
(for 10 persons)

Freshly-salted whitefish
New potatoes
Butter sauce

Rantakala
Rye bread

Rhubarb pudding
Whipped cream

Late-night supper
(for 10 persons)

Smoked ham
Summer salad
Grandma's salad dressing

The arrangement is like a Midsummer Eve bride — white and blue.
The white, delicate dishes and bird-patterned tablecloth fit in well with the lake-side setting. The eating utensils and napkins are set out in a novel way — in two matching bowls.

Freshly-salted whitefish
Preparation time: about 20 minutes
Salting time: 1–3 days
Suitable for freezing

about 3 lb. (1 1/2 kg)
cleaned whitefish
4 tablespoons sea salt
2 tablespoons sugar
about 15 white peppercorns
fresh dill

1. Wipe the cleaned fish with a paper towel without rinsing, fillet.
2. Grind the peppercorns and mix with the salt and sugar. Rub the fillets with the mixture, place some dill between each pair of fillets, skin-side out. Sprinkle some of the mixture over the bottom of the dish. Arrange the fillets in the dish and cover with aluminium foil and a small weight. Store in a cool place.
3. The fish are ready to be eaten the next day. Cut the fillets into thin, oblique slices and garnish with dill. Will keep for a week if stored in the refrigerator.

Hint
The heads, backbones and fins will make an excellent fish stock. Put all the fish scraps in a little cold water and bring to boil. Skim off the foam as it forms. Add a few peppercorns, a bay leaf and a halved onion. Simmer gently for about one hour. Strain, thicken and add salt to taste. Makes a tasty starter or can be used to make fish stews.

New potatoes
Preparation time: about 15 minutes
Cooking time: about 20 minutes
Not suitable for freezing

4 1/2 lb. (2 kg) new potatoes
1 tablespoon salt
fresh dill

1. Scrub the potatoes with a stiff brush.
2. Place in salty boiling water and cook with the lid on for 20 minutes.
3. Pour off the water, put the saucepan back onto the heat until the steam has dispersed.
4. Garnish just before serving with fresh dill.

Butter sauce for the potatoes
Preparation time: about 10 minutes

5 oz. (150 g) butter
1/2 cup(3/4 dl) milk
1 teaspoon salt
fresh dill

Melt the butter in a saucepan and add the milk and salt. Bring it to a boil and season with finely-chopped dill.

Rantakala
Preparation time: about 1 hour
Cooking time: 1–1 1/2 hours
Suitable for freezing

6 1/2 lb. (3 kg) vendace, smelt or other small fish
8 oz. (150–300 g) butter
1 3/4 cups (3–4 dl) water
6 teaspoons salt
about 15 whole allspice
some chives or 1 onion

Rantakala is prepared in a ceramic chafingdish on a stove or over an open fire. The fish is served straight from the dish and kept hot and tasty at the table on a small burner.

1. Clean the fish. This is best done by removing the gills and pulling out the gut without cutting through the belly. Rinse the fish under the tap and leave to drain.
2. Put the fish into the heated mixture of water, butter, allspice, salt and finely-chopped chives or onion.
3. Leave the fish to cook slowly on a low heat, on hot coals out-doors or in a slow oven at 300 °F (150 °C) for at least one hour.

Hint
This dish is traditionally served with rye bread alone. The bread is dunked in the broth to bring out the rich taste of the cooked fish. Boiled potatoes can also be served with this dish.

Rhubarb pudding
Preparation time: about 10 minutes
Cooking time: 30 minutes

6 cups (1 1/2 l) rhubarb
1 cup (2 dl) sugar
4 cups (1 l) water
4 tablespoons potato starch
Topping: 2 dl whipping cream
1 tablespoon sugar

1. Rinse the rhubarb and cut up into short sections. There is no need to peel the stalks.
2. Put the sugar and rhubarb in layers in an enamel or steel saucepan. Add a small amount of water. Simmer the rhubarb on very low heat, or put in a slow oven at 300 °F (150 °C) for half an hour.
3. Add the water and bring to a boil.
4. Mix the potato starch in a small amount of water, take the pan off the heat and stir in the well-mixed potato starch thickener. Put the pan back on the heat and bring to a boil without stirring.
5. Pour the stewed rhubarb into a serving dish and sprinkle with a little sugar to prevent a skin forming, or cover with plastic wrap. For special occasions, top with whipped cream.
    NOTE: keep the pudding at room temperature; its color and consistency may change if kept in a refrigerator.

Fruit pudding is served as tradition demands in a shallow dish.

Hint
If you want a dessert which is not thick, reduce the amount of potato starch by half.

Smoked ham
4 1/2 lb. (about 2 kg) smoked ham

Offer the smoked ham for a midnight snack. Make scores in the skin beforehand — this will give it an attractive appearance and make it easier to carve at the table.

Summer salad
Preparation time: about 20 minutes

3 heads of lettuce
10 tomatoes
chopped chives
medium-sized cucumber
fresh dill

1. Rinse the vegetables and leave to drain.
2. Shred the lettuce, quarter the tomatoes and thinly slice the cucumber.
3. Put the vegetables in layers in a salad bowl. Finely-chopped chives should be sprinkled over the tomatoes, and finely-chopped dill over the cucumber.
4. Use the following good old recipe for the salad dressing served with the salad.

Grandma's salad dressing
Preparation time: about 10 minutes

3/4 cups (2 dl) whipping cream
2 tablespoons vinegar
1 1/2 teaspoons sugar
1/2 teaspoon salt
1/2 tablespoon prepared mustard
pinch of white pepper
2 eggs

1. Hard-boil the eggs (about 10 min.). Cool in cold water. Shell the eggs and separate the white from the yolks.
2. Mash the yolks with a fork and add the vinegar, sugar, salt, mustard and pepper. Whip the cream and blend into the mixture.
3. Pour over the salad and garnish with the finely-chopped egg whites.

Garden Party in the Summer

Finns spend much of their time in the summer at their country cottages. Guests are very welcome, unexpected ones usually bring some summer delicacies with them. The food served is light and simple. Raw vegetables make an ideal starter, followed by a traditional Finnish delicacy: fish soup and warm rye bread. Dessert is easily-prepared strawberry flan, which no one can resist.

Summer evening
(for 10 persons)

Summer vegetable platter

Fish soup
Rye bread

Strawberry flan
Coffee

Summer vegetable platter
Cauliflower
Carrots
Peas in the pod
Cucumbers
Tomatoes
Turnips
Radishes

Rinse the vegetables and cut them up into suitable sized pieces. You can serve them with different types of dips or sauces, e.g. sour cream flavored with dill and chives, grated onion and apple, or leek.

Finnish fish soup
Preparation time: about 30 minutes
Cooking time: about 1 hour
Not suitable for freezing

3 1/4 lb. (1 1/2 kg) perch or other freshwater fish
9 cups (2 l) water
3 1/4 lb. (1 1/2 kg) potatoes
2 medium-sized onions or 1 leek
15 whole allspice or blackpepper
1 bay leaf
5 tablespoons butter
1 tablespoon salt
1 1/2 cups (4 dl) sour cream
fresh dill or green part of a leek

1. Clean the fish and cut into chunks. Peel and cut up the potatoes.
2. Put the potatoes on the bottom of the pan and cover with the sliced onions or leeks and the spices. Place the fish on top, add the butter and cover with lukewarm water. NOTE: high altitude: boil potatoes half done and then add fish.
3. Bring to a boil and leave to simmer over a low heat.
4. Just before serving add the sour cream, stir and check the seasoning.
5. Garnish with the chopped dill or green leek tops and bring to the table.
6. Serve with warm rye bread.

Strawberry flan
Preparation time: 20 minutes
Baking time: 25–30 minutes
Oven temperature: 350 °F (180°C)
Suitable for freezing

5 oz. (150 g) margarine
1/2 cup (1 dl) sugar
1 egg
1 1/4 cup (200 g, 3 dl) white flour
1 teaspoon baking powder
Filling: 1 quart (1 l) strawberries
1/2 cup (1 dl) sugar

1. Cream the softened margarine and sugar until light and fluffy. Beat in the egg.
2. Mix the baking powder into the flour and add to the mix. Line the bottom and sides of the baking dish with the pastry.
3. Spread the strawberries in the baking dish, cutting any really large ones in half. Sprinkle with the sugar.
4. If you want to decorate the flan with strips of pastry, reserve some pastry dough when lining the baking dish. Roll out into thin strips on waxed paper and arrange them cross-wise over the flan.
5. Cook in the oven until the pastry is golden brown.

The colors on the table compete with those of nature. The table cloth is summery and chequered, the dinner service at the summer cottage being white and simple. The enamel pan can be lifted straight from the cooker onto the table: the food keeps looking its best and saves work for the hostess. The coffee cups can be stacked on top of each other and are ideally suited for the cramped cupboards of a summer cottage (on the left).

Autumn Fish Festival

The Baltic herring, the most commonly-used fish in Finnish cooking, is ideally suited for everyday meals and for special occasions. Small herrings or smelts, 10–15 cm long, can be substituted in all the following recipes. It is served in many different ways — freshly-salted, grilled, smoked, poached or fried. The guests can participate in preparing the dishes throughout the evening.

Fish buffet
(for 10 persons)

Cobbler's salmon
Rolled fish
Barbecued fish
Stuffed fish fillets
Fish pie
Smoked fish flan
Fish and potato casserole
Easy fish and potato pot
Small boiled beets

Rye bread
Butter

Cleaning fish

The easiest way to prepare these dishes is of course to use ready-filleted smelts. 1 1/3 lb. (about 600 g) filleted smelts is equivalent to 2 1/4 lbs. (1 kg) of unfilleted. The simplest way to clean them is by removing the gills and gut by hand. If the heads are to be removed this is easily done by twisting them off and pulling out the gut at the same time. Of course scissors can also be used, but doing the job by hand is by far the quickest method.

Smelt dishes are not really suitable for freezing.

Cobbler's salmon
Soaking time: 3–5 hours
Preparation time: 30 minutes
Marinading time: 1–2 days

2 1/4 lb. (1 kg) salted smelts
10 whole allspice or black pepper
1 onion
1 bay leaf
Marinade: 3/4 cup (2 dl) water
1/3 cup (1 dl) white vinegar or equivalent
2 1/2 lb. (1/2 dl) sugar

1. Soak the smelts in cold water for a few hours. Boil up the marinade liquid and leave to cool.
2. Clean, fillet and split each smelt into two fillets. Peel and slice the onions, grind up the allspice.
3. Arrange the fillets and spices in layers in a deep serving dish, pour over the liquid. Leave in a cool place to marinade.

Hint
This dish can also be prepared using fresh smelts.

2 1/4 lb. (1 kg) smelts
2 tablespoons coarse salt

Rub the salt over the fresh, cleaned smelts. Leave them in a cool place for 1–2 days under a light weight. Fillet and prepare as above.

Rolled fish
Preparation time: about 40 minutes
Cooking time: 10–15 minutes

2 1/4 lb. (1 kg) smelts or herrings
2 bunches of chives
2 teaspoons salt
1 onion
a few white peppercorns
Cooking liquid: 2 1/2 lb. (1/2 dl) vinegar or equivalent
3/4 cup (2 dl) water
2 teaspoons sugar
2 teaspoons salt

1. Clean and fillet the smelts. Season the fillets with salt and sprinkle with chopped chives.
2. Roll up, and arrange in lines on the bottom of a shallow baking dish.
3. Prepare the cooking liquid by mixing the vinegar, water, salt and sugar together. Pour over the fish rolls. Top with onion rings and peppercorns.
4. Bake in a moderate oven.

Rolled smelts can be served either hot or cold.

Barbecued fish
Preparation time: 30 minutes
Salting time: about 2 hours
Grilling time: 8–10 minutes/batch

2 1/4 lb. (1 kg) smelts or snall herrings
1 teaspoon coarse salt
white pepper
cooking oil

1. Clean and rinse the fish.
2. Carefully dry the fish, rub with the seasoning and leave for a couple of hours. The fish can also be seasoned after cooking.
3. Place the fish side-by-side on the rack of the grill. Cook the fish over the coals of the grill or open fire.

Stuffed fish fillets
Preparation time: about 1 hour
Frying time: about 15 minutes

4 1/2 lb. (2 kg) herrings or smelts
Filling: 4 teaspoons salt
white pepper
fresh dill
Coating: 3/4 cup (2 dl) rye flour
1 teaspoon salt
oil, margarine or butter for frying

1. Clean the fish, rinse quickly and remove the backbones.
2. Spread out half of the fish on the work surface, skin side down, and sprinkle with salt, white pepper and plenty of finely-chopped dill.

The board for the fish table is an old, weather-beaten boathouse door. It goes together with the food so well that a table cloth is quite superfluous. All the serving dishes have lids so that any left-overs can easily be stored as they are. No flowers are needed, just a few small candles. The napkins get their color from the apples, red onions and beets.

As a balance to the dark serving dishes, simple but attractive looking glass plates are well suited for eating outdoors.

Place the other half of the fish on top and press together lightly.
3. Mix the rye flour and salt together and coat the fish steaks with the mixture. Fry the steaks over medium heat until evenly browned.

NOTE: the steaks can also be cooked in the oven at 390 °F (200 °C).

Hint

Other fillings, such as anchovies, finely-chopped chives or leek, go perfectly with smelts or herrings. The steaks are also very tasty served cold.

Fish pie
Preparation time: about 1 hour
Baking time: 1–1 1/2 hours
Oven temperature: 350 °F (175 °C)

Potato pastry: 1 1/2 cups (300 g) butter or margarine
1 1/2 cups (300 g) cooked and mashed potatoes
1 1/2 cups (300 g) flour (5 dl)
1 teaspoon salt
Filling: 4 eggs
1/3 cup (1/2–1 dl) rice
1 fish bouillon cube
2 1/4 lb. (1 kg) filleted smelts or herrings
3 teaspoons salt
1 teaspoon white pepper
2 bunches of fresh dill

1. Cook the rice for the filling in the fish stock.
2. Hard-boil the eggs (10–12 min-

utes). Mash the eggs with a fork. Chop up the dill.
3. Mix the ingredients for the potato pastry as quickly as possible to prevent it from becoming tough. Let the dough rest in a cold place for a while.
4. Divide the pastry into two and roll out to form two circles, one slightly larger than the other. Line the bottom and sides of the baking dish with the larger piece.
5. Fill the dish with alternate layers of rice, fish fillets, chopped egg, dill and the seasoning.
6. Cover the dish with the rest of the pastry and brush with beaten egg. Prick lightly with a fork and put in the oven to bake.

Serve it as it is or with dill-flavored melted butter.

Smoked fish flan
Preparation time: 30 minutes
Baking time: 30–40 minutes
Oven temperature: 350 °F (175 °C)

2 1/4 lb. (1 kg) smoked small fish
1 bunch of chives
1 bunch of fresh dill
4 eggs
1 1/2 cups (4 dl) milk

1. Clean the fish, remove the skin and backbone.
2. Place the fillets in a greased baking dish and sprinkle with finely-chopped dill and chives.
3. Lightly whip the eggs and milk, pour over the fish. Bake.

Fish and potato casserole
Preparation time: 40 minutes
Soaking time: 2–3 hours
Cooking time: 1 1/2–2 hours
Oven temperature: 350 °F (175 °C)

15 salted smelts or herrings
2 1/4 lb. (2 kg) potatoes
1 oz (200 g) fresh side of pork
3 onions
4 cups (1 l) milk
3 eggs
2 tablespoons white flour
1/2 teaspoon white pepper

1. Soak and clean the fish, removing the backbone.
2. Peel and slice the potatoes.

14

Chop up the onions and fry until transparent.

3. Cut up the pork into thin slices. They can be fried before adding to the casserole.

4. Fill a large baking dish with alternate layers of sliced potatoes, fish fillets (skin side down), onion and sliced pork, starting and finishing with potatoes.

5. Combine the lightly-beaten eggs, milk and flour, pour over the other ingredients and place in the oven.

One traditional Finnish herring dish is prepared by steaming the salted herrings or smelts on top of the potatoes boiled in their jackets.

Easy fish and potato pot

Preparation time: 10 minutes
Soaking time: 2–3 hours
Cooking time: 30 minutes

1 lb. (1/2 kg) salted smelts or herrings
2 1/4 lb. (1 kg) potatoes
water

1. Soak the fish in cold water.

2. Scrub the potatoes and cut in half. Place the potatoes in a deep baking dish, lay the fish on top and add the water. Place in the oven.

Hint

Freshly-salted fish can also be used instead, without soaking.

Small boiled beets

Preparation time: 10 minutes
Cooking time: 20–30 minutes

4 1/2 lb. (2 kg) small beets
salt, water
Dressing: 2 tablespoons cooking oil
4 tablespoons lemon juice
1/2 teaspoon salt

1. Scrub the beets but do not remove the roots so that they retain their color and flavor.

2. Place the beets in slightly-salted boiling water and cook until tender. When ready rinse immediately in cold water and remove the skins.

3. Mix the ingredients for the dressing sauce together and pour over the cooked beets.

Christmas Time

Christmas in Finland starts with rice or barley porridge which is eaten on Christmas Eve morning. The easiest way is to bake it in the oven.

Christmas porridge on Christmas eve morning
(for 10 persons)

Rice porridge

A hot drink for the afternoon
(for 10 persons)

Homemade spiced punch

As the traditional Christmas Eve dinner is eaten late in the afternoon, it is worth starting the day with sustaining, delicious rice porridge.

Rice porridge
(for 10 persons)
Preparation time: 10 minutes
Cooking time: 40 minutes
Suitable for freezing

2 cups (1/2 l) water
6 cups (1 1/2 l) milk
1 1/4 cups (3 dl) rice
2 1/2 teaspoons salt
1 almond

1. Add the rice to the boiling milk and water mixture.
2. Simmer until cooked. Add the salt and one almond. Serve with ground cinnamon, sugar to taste, and milk.

Hint
If there is any porridge left over, you can make a delicious pudding out of it. Add an egg, raisins, a little sugar and a few drops of vanilla extract. Pour the mixture into a greased dish and add a few dabs of butter or margarine. Cook in the

oven for half an hour at about 380 °F (200 °C). Serve with thick lingonberry pudding (see p. 62), berry fruit soup or jam.

Alternative
Baked barley porridge
(for 10 persons)
Preparation time: 5 minutes
Cooking time: about 1 hour
Slow baking time: overnight
Heating-up time: 20–30 minutes
Oven temperature: 350 °F (175 °C)
Suitable for freezing

4 cups (1 l) water
4 cups (1 l) milk
1 1/4 cups (3 dl) whole pearl barley
2 1/2 teaspoons salt
1 tablespoon butter or margarine for greasing the baking dish

1. Grease one large or two small baking dishes.
2. Put all the ingredients in the dish and mix well.
3. Cook in the oven for about one hour.

4. Turn off the oven, cover with a lid or aluminium foil and leave in the oven overnight.
5. The porridge will still be slightly warm in the morning but heat it up in the oven before serving.

This is a very easy way of preparing a baked porridge. Serve with milk, sugar and ground cinnamon.

Homemade spiced punch
Preparation time: 10 minutes

2 1/2 cups (6 dl) blackcurrant juice
2 1/2 cups (6 dl) water
2 teaspoons of a mixture of ground cinnamon, ginger, cloves and cardamom
blanched almonds
raisins

Mix the water, blackcurrant juice and spices together and heat up. Do not boil. Put a few raisins and an almond in each guest's glass and pour over the punch.

This is a very tasty and warming drink which can be offered on other occasions, too.

Hint
It is easier to peel the almonds if they are immersed for a moment in boiling water.

A novel, personal touch for the Christmas table: the candles are standing in sand in an earthenware bowl (on the left).

Christmas porridge can be served in the kitchen so that the dining table can be set in the morning, ready for the Christmas Eve dinner. Quilt batting and ever-lasting flowers, sprigs of juniper and lingonberry placed between the window frames make attractive Christmas decorations in city homes. Rosolli makes a savory pick-you-up on Christmas morning instead of being served on Christmas Eve (on the right).

Christmas Time

Christmas is the most traditional of Finnish festivals. It is a time for the family, close relatives, friends without family, but above all for the children. The good old traditional dishes appear on the Christmas dining table year after year. Casserole dishes — Finnish cuisine at its best — can easily be made a few days beforehand.

Traditional Christmas eve dinner
(for 10 persons)

Freshly-salted salmon
Glass Master's herring
Boiled potatoes
Rosolli (see p. 54)
Salad cream (see p. 55)
Liver pâté
Egg cheese

Baked ham
Rutabaga casserole
Mashed potato casserole
Red cabbage and blackcurrant salad

Mixed fruit soup

Milk
Mineral water
Juniper beer
Christmas rye bread

Freshly-salted salmon
Preparation time: about 25 minutes
Salting time: 1–3 days
Not suitable for freezing

Large piece of salmon, about 4 1/2 lb. (2 kg)
1/3 cup (1 dl) coarse salt
4 tablespoons sugar
3–4 teaspoons roughly-ground white pepper
plenty of fresh dill

1. Fillet the salmon unless bought already filleted. Do not, however, remove the skin.
2. Wipe the fillets with paper towels without rinsing.
3. Sprinkle the bottom of a suitable-sized dish with salt and place one of the fillets, skin side down, on top. Spread the seasoning over both the fillets, placing the other fillet, skin side up, on top. Sprinkle the rest of the salt and the dill over the fish. Cover the dish tightly with aluminium foil. Put a small weight on top and store in a cool place.
4. Scrape off all the seasoning and cut the fillets down to the skin into thin, oblique slices before serving.

Hint
Freshly-salted salmon does not require any sort of dressing, especially when served at Christmas. However, mustard dressing goes very well with this dish.

Prepare as follows just before serving the salmon: Mix together 3 tablespoons darkish prepared mustard, 2 tablespoons sugar and 4 tablespoons wine vinegar. Add 3/4 cup (2 dl) oil, preferably olive oil, in a thin stream while beating at the same time. Last of all, mix in plenty of finely-chopped fresh dill.

Glass master's herring
Preparation time: 30 minutes
Soaking time: 12 hours
Marinading time: 2–3 days

4 good-sized herrings
3 red onions
2 carrots
30 whole allspice and white peppercorns
4 bay leaves
Marinade: 1 1/4 cup (3 dl) vinegar
1 1/4 cup (3 dl) sugar
2 1/2 cups (6 dl) water

1. Soak the fish overnight in cold water or equal portions of water and milk. The liquid can be changed occasionally.
2. Prepare the marinade: boil up all the ingredients and leave to cool at room temperature.
3. Remove the gut and inside belly membrane with, for instance, kitchen scissors. Rinse well and dry with paper towels. Cut up into shortish sections.
4. Peel the onions and carrots and cut into rings.
5. Fill a suitable glass jar with alternate layers of fish slices, onions and carrots, and the spices. Pour over the liquid.
6. Cover the jar and store in a cool place for at least two days. The herrings will keep for a couple of weeks in a cool place, but they are at their best after 4–5 days.

Hint
Different spices can also be used: thin slices of horseradish or celery seeds, mustard seeds, cloves.

The fish can also be filleted and the skin removed. Soaking is not then required.

Liver pâté
Preparation time: 30 minutes
Cooking time: 2 hours
Oven temperature: 350 °F (175 °C)
Not suitable for freezing

1 lb. (1/2 kg) ground liver
3/4 cup (2 dl) dried breadcrumbs
1 1/2 cup (4 dl) cream
2 onions
2 tablespoons butter
4 tablespoons potato starch
3 teaspoons salt
1 teaspoon sugar
1 teaspoon ground ginger
1 teaspoon white pepper
2 eggs
fresh side of pork

1. Line an oblong baking dish with fresh side of pork. When buying the liver ask your butcher to grind it twice.

A deep red, roughly-woven table cloth with a soft, living surface that is as if created for stoneware dishes, provides the perfect base for an intimate and genuine Christmas table setting. The colour of the cloth is repeated in the rosolli, candles and napkins and the small hearts on the Christmas tree. The cold-cut dishes are served in identical, roasting pans arranged t form a line.

2. Mix the cream and dried bread-crumbs and leave to swell.

3. Finely chop the onions and fry in butter until transparent. Leave to cool.

4. Mix together the liver and other ingredients, finishing with the light-ly beaten eggs. Blend together thor-oughly.

5. Pour the mixture into the baking dish, cover tightly with aluminium foil. Set in a pan of water and bake in the oven.

Egg cheese or buttermilk cheese
(makes 1 large cheese)
Preparation time: 25 minutes
Draining time: 6–12 hours
Suitable for freezing

16 cups (4 l) milk
6 cups (1 1/2 l) buttermilk
4 eggs
1 tablespoon salt

1. Boil the milk in a heavy-bottomed kettle.

2. Mix together the egg whites, buttermilk and salt.

3. Add the mixture to the hot milk and stir well.

4. Bring the mixture back to the boiling point to separate the cheese curds. Take the pan off the heat and keep at room temperature until the mixture curdles completely.

5. Transfer the cheese curds to a sieve using a slotted spoon. Leave to drain for five minutes.

6. Pour the curds into a bowl and mix in the egg yolks.

7. Line a cheese mould with damp cheesecloth and fill with the cheese curds. Fold the edges of the cheese-cloth over the top of the cheese.

8. Leave the cheese to drain over-night and then invert it onto a serving dish.

Hint 1
If you do not have a cheese mold one can easily be made by lining a kitchen colander with cheese cloth.

Hint 2
Egg cheese also makes a delicious dessert when served with fresh or frozen berries, or jam.

Baked ham
Preparation time: 10 minutes
Cooking time: 45–55 minutes/2 lb. (1 kg)
Oven temperature: 250–300 °F (125–150) and 440 °F (225 °C)

ready-salted ham 10–15 lb. (5–8 kg)
Coating: 2–4 tablespoons home-made mustard (see below)
2–4 tablespoons brown sugar
2–4 tablespoons dried bread-crumbs
cloves for decorating

1. Place the ham on a wiregrid in the roasting pan, skin side up. Push a roasting thermometer into the thickest part of the ham making sure it does not touch the bone.

2. Put the ham in the oven. It is difficult to give a precise roasting time, it is best to go by the roasting thermometer. When it reaches 170 °F (77 °C) the meat is cooked.

3. Remove from the oven and let it stand for a moment. Remove the skin and as much of the underlying fat as required.

4. Mix together the ingredients for the coating and smear over the ham. Put back into the oven at 440 °F (225 °C) for ten minutes or until golden brown all over. Decorate the surface of the ham with the cloves.

NOTE: if the ham is cooked at a lower temperature less liquid will be lost and the meat will be much more succulent. Of course the lower the temperature, the longer the cooking time.

Variation
Many people consider that the meat will be much juicier if the ham is covered with a pastry crust. Pre-pare the pastry by mixing about 2 cups (800 g) rye flour in one litre of water. The pastry is then rolled out or patted over the surface of the ham to give a crust about 1/2 inch (1 1/2 cm) thick. No salt should be added to the pastry. If the ham happens to be too salty, the pastry crust will absorb the excess salt.

Hint
The meat juices which collect in the roasting pan can be used to make a tasty gravy. Be careful, however, it will be rather salty. One well-tried method is to mix in some apple sauce, flavour with ground ginger and mustard, and serve together with the warm ham.

Homemade mustard
Preparation time: 10 minutes
Cooking time: about 5 minutes

1/3 cup (1 dl) mustard powder
1/3 cup (1 dl) sugar
(1/3 cup (1 dl) cream
1/3 cup (1 dl) egg yolks
1 teaspoon potato starch
2 teaspoons vinegar
dash of salt

1. Blend the mustard powder and sugar together.

2. Add the egg yolks, cream and potato starch.

3. Heat until it boils, stirring con-tinuously.

4. Add the salt and vinegar after the mixture has cooled.

NOTE: homemade mustard will keep for weeks.

Casseroles
Casserole dishes form the main part of the hot dishes served at Christ-mas. They are very useful from the hostesses' point of view because they can be prepared well in ad-vance. They keep well for two or three days when stored in a cool place — the flavor of the rutabaga casserole, for instance, improves with reheating.

Homemade casseroles are Fin-nish cuisine at its best: nutritious and much easier to prepare than one would imagine and also excep-tionally economical.

Rutabaga casserole
Preparation time: 25–30 minutes
Boiling time for the rutabagas 30–40 minutes
Cooking time: 1 1/2–2 hours
Oven temperature: 350 °F (175 °C)
Suitable for freezing

2 large rutabagas, 3 1/2 lb. (about 1 1/2 kg)
1 1/2 cups (4 dl) cream or mixture

of cream and milk
3/4 cup (2 dl) dried breadcrumbs
1/3 cup (1 dl) dark syrup
1 egg
1 1/2 teaspoons ground ginger
1/2 teaspoon white pepper
1/2 teaspoon grated nutmeg
1 tablespoon salt
Coating: dried breadcrumbs,
butter

1. Scrub and peel the rutabagas. Cut up into large pieces and boil in slightly-salted water until soft.
2. Strain, keep the cooking liquid, and mash or blend the rutabagas in a kitchen blender.
3. Mix in the cream and dried breadcrumb paste, dark syrup, beaten egg and spices, and as much of the cooking liquid as is needed to give a loose soft consistency.
4. Turn into a greased baking dish, press the surface with a fork to make a pattern, sprinkle over a thin coating of dried breadcrumbs.
5. Dot the top with butter and bake in the oven.
   NOTE: The flavor of the rutabaga casserole can be further enhanced by adding some lightly-fried, grated onion.

Mashed potato casserole
Preparation time: 10 minutes + 25 minutes
Malting time: 12 hours
Cooking time: 2 1/2–3 hours
Oven temperature: 300 °F (150 °C)
Not suitable for freezing

5 3/4 lb. (2 1/2 kg) potatoes
1/2 cup (100 g) butter
1 tablespoon salt
3 tablespoons white flour
28 oz. (7–9 dl) milk
2 teaspoons ground ginger
(1 teaspoon grated nutmeg)
Coating: dried breadcrumbs,
butter

1. Peel the potatoes and boil in unsalted water until soft.
2. Drain and mash thoroughly.
3. Add the butter and half of the flour. Sprinkle the rest of the flour over the surface of the mixture.
4. Cover with a lid and leave to malt overnight in a warm place. If

you are in a hurry, 3–4 hours should be suffcient.
5. Add the milk, stirring vigorously to give a smooth paste.
6. Add the salt and ginger (and the nutmeg if desired).
7. Turn into a greased baking dish, leaving room for the mixture to rise during baking.
8. Sprinkle dried breadcrumbs over the surface and dot with butter.
9. Bake in the oven until golden brown on top. Serve hot.

Red cabbage and blackcurrant salad
Preparation time: 20 minutes

about 3 cups (600 g) red cabbage
1 1/4 cups (3 dl) blackcurrant jam or frozen blackcurrants (add a little sugar when using frozen berries)

1. Slice the cabbage finely or grate using a coarse grater.
2. Mash the blackcurrants if using frozen ones.
3. Mix together and leave to stand in a cool place for a few hours before serving.

Mixed fruit soup
Preparation time: 5 minutes
Soaking time: overnight
Cooking time: about 15 minutes

about 1 lb. (400 g) dried mixed fruit
8 cups (2 l) water
3/4 cup (1 1/2 dl) sugar
stick of cinnamon
(dash of salt)
3 tablespoons potato starch

1. Rinse the mixed fruit in cold water and leave to soak overnight in water containing a little sugar.
2. Boil the fruit in the soaking liquid with the cinnamon and a touch of salt if desired.
3. Continue to boil over a low heat until the fruit is fully cooked.
4. Transfer the fruit with a slotted spoon to the serving dish and remove the stick of cinnamon.
5. Thicken the juice: remove the pan from the heat, mix the potato starch in a little cold water and add in a thin stream to the liquid, stir-

ring continuously. Bring quickly back to a boil without stirring.
6. Pour over the fruit and sprinkle a little sugar over the top.

Juniper beer
Preparation time: 15 minutes
Fermenting time: 1 day + 2 days

3 cups (8 dl) dried malt flour
1 1/2 cups (4 dl) sugar
32 cups (8 l) water
a few sprigs of juniper
1 teaspoon yeast

1. Put the water and rinsed juniper sprigs in a saucepan. Bring to a boil.
2. Strain the liquid and pour over the malt and sugar.
3. Leave to stand until lukewarm and then add the yeast dissolved in a little water.
4. Leave to ferment for one day and then strain and bottle.
The beer is ready to be served after a couple of days.

Christmas rye bread
(makes 3 loaves)
Preparation time: 30 minutes
Rising time: 1 1/2 hours altogether
Baking time: about 40 minutes
Oven temperature: 400 °F (200 °C)
Suitable for freezing

4 cups (1 l) buttermilk
2 oz. (50 g) yeast
3/4 cup (2 dl) dark syrup
2 tablespoons grated orange peel
1/2 tablespoon roughly ground caraway seeds
1 tablespoon salt
about 3 cups (8 dl) rye flour
1 1/2 cups (4 dl) graham flour
about 4 cups (1 l) white flour

1. Warm up the buttermilk.
2. Crumble in the yeast and add the syrup and spices.
3. Mix in the flour and knead thoroughly. Cover with a cloth and leave to rise. If the kitchen is drafty, stand the covered bowl in warmish water.
4. Divide the dough into three and shape each portion into a round loaf. Put in a warm place to rise. Prick with a fork before placing in the oven.

Christmas Time

By tradition, Grandma prepares the Christmas coffee table. The guests are met at the door by the fragrant aroma of freshly-baked Christmas buns and the finest coffee. This is an ideal time when everyone, from the oldest to the youngest in the family, can get together to sing Christmas carols and play games.

Grandma's Christmas coffee table
(for 10 persons)

Christmas buns
Fruit cake
Christmas star
Grandma's best ginger cookies
Coffee

Christmas buns
Saffron can be used to give the dough used for Christmas buns (see p. 48) a beautiful color. Add a little saffron to 1/4 teaspoon lukewarm milk.

Fruit cake
Preparation time: 30 minutes
Cooking time: 50–60 minutes
Oven temperature: 350 °F (175 °C)
Suitable for freezing

1 cup (200 g) margarine at room temperature
1 cup (2 1/2 dl) sugar
3 eggs
1 1/2 cup (250 g) white flour
1/3 cup (1 dl) raisins
3 tablespoons finely-chopped, candied orange peel

A precious, heirloom silk table-cloth, gold-edged cups, white begonia and a Christmas elf which has been in hiding for a year, decorate the coffee table. Old-fashioned cake dishes and candlesticks give a fine finish to the arrangement.

2 tablespoons finely-chopped candied Fruit Cake Mix
1/4 cup (1/2 dl) finely-chopped almonds
2 teaspoons baking powder

1. Cream the margarine and sugar until soft and add the eggs one at a time. Beat well.
2. Mix the raisins, candied fruit and baking powder with a little flour to prevent them from sinking to the bottom during baking.
3. Add the flour, fruit and chopped almonds to the mixture.
4. Pour into a greased baking tin coated with dried bread crumbs and bake in the oven for about one hour until done.
5. Cool slightly before removing from the baking tin.

Christmas star
Preparation time: 20 minutes
Resting time for pastry: at least 1 hour + overnight
Cooking time: 20 minutes
Oven temperature: 400 °F (200 °C)
The uncooked pastry can be frozen

Puff pastry:
1 1/2 cups (250 g) white flour (about 4 dl)
1/3 cup (1 dl) water
1 1/4 cups (250 g) butter or margarine
Filling: 3/4 cup (2 dl) cream
1 tablespoon sugar
juice of half a lemon
300 g apple or prune purée
(slices of apple for decorating)

1. Mix together the flour and water but do not beat.
2. Divide the butter or margarine when soft into three portions. Roll out the dough into a large oblong.
3. Spread one of the portions of butter over the dough right up to the edges. Fold over to give three layers.
4. Leave the dough to rest for about one hour at room temperature.
5. Roll out the dough into a large oblong again and repeat as in Point 3.
6. Leave the dough to rest for some time and repeat as in Point 3, adding the final portion of butter.
7. All this should be done in the

evening and the dough then left overnight in the refrigerator.
8. Roll out the dough into a 1/2 cm-thick oblong.
9. Cut out a large star from baking paper, place on top of the dough and cut round the edges with a knife or pastry wheel. Make two pastry stars.
10. Prick the stars all over with a fork and brush the stars with beaten egg, except the edges as it prevents the pastry from rising in the oven. Bake in the oven. Leave to cool. Put the filling between the stars just before serving, as otherwise the pastry will become tough.
11. Whip the cream for the filling and add the sugar and lemon juice.
12. Place one of the stars on a serving dish. Fill up the centre with the prune or apple purée, followed by the cream, and then place the other star on top.

Grandma's best ginger cookies
(makes about 200)
Preparation time: 30 minutes
Cooking time: 10 minutes/batch
Oven temperature: 400 °F (200 °C)

1 1/4 cups (300 g) margarine
1 1/4 cups (300 g) sugar
3 eggs
1 cup (250 g) dark syrup
2 teaspoons ground cinnamon
2 teaspoons ground ginger
2 teaspoons ground cloves
1 tablespoon grated orange rind
about 7 cups (1 kg) white flour
3 teaspoons bicarbonate of soda

1. Boil the syrup and spices, add the margarine and beat until the mixture is cool.
2. Beat the eggs and sugar.
3. Mix the soda in with part of the flour and then combine with the syrup-margarine mixture. Add the whipped eggs and the rest of the flour. Do not knead the final mixture.
4. Cover the dough with plastic wrap and leave overnight in a cool place.
5. Roll out the dough, cut up into shapes and bake the cookies in the oven until golden brown.

Christmas Time

Boxing Day is traditionally spent visiting friends and relatives. Light meals are usually served. A salad, based on ham, makes a refreshing opener. Lutefisk is always served at Christmas time and here this delicacy has been reserved for Boxing Day. The meal is finished off with cranberry parfait.

Boxing day
(for 10 persons)

Celery and ham salad

Lutefisk
White sauce
Boiled potatoes

Cranberry parfait

Celery and ham salad
Preparation time: about 40 minutes

4 celerystalks
4 apples
1 3/4 cups (about 400 g) leftover ham
1 small leek

The translucent blue of winter, blue and whitechecked cotton table cloth and blue and white dinner service create a serene atmosphere. Small napkins for the side plates have been cut from the same cloth. The salad is served in small individual bowls. The napkins repeat the same pattern as the table cloth, but in white. The knives and forks are rolled up in the napkins. The serving dish for the frozen cranberry parfait and the flower vase are made of white filigree glass. The whole table reflects the spirit of winter — the empty spaces on the table show off the tablecloth.

Dressing: 1/3 cup (3/4 dl) cooking oil
1/4 cup (1/2 dl) lemon juice
1 1/2 teaspoons sugar
1/4 teaspoon salt
1/4 teaspoon white pepper
(1 teaspoon mustard)

1. Cut the celery finely. Cut up the ham and apples into thin matchsticks. Mix together and add the chopped leek.
3. Measure the ingredients for the dressing into a small bottle. Cover tightly and shake vigorously until well mixed and slightly thickened.
4. Pour the dressing over the salad and toss gently using two forks.

Baked lutefisk
Preparation time: 10 minutes
Cooking time: 40–50 minutes
Oven temperature: 400 °F (200 °C)

5 to 6 lb. (2–3 kg) lutefisk
1 1/2 tablespoons salt

1. Set the pieces of fish on aluminium foil or roasting film and sprinkle with salt. Wrap up tightly.
2. Place in a ceramic baking dish or enamel pan.
3. Bake in the oven for 40–50 minutes depending on the amount of fish.
4. Discard the liquid formed in the packet.
Serve with boiled potatoes and white sauce seasoned with freshly-ground allspice or white pepper and salt.

Variation
Boiled lutefisk
Preparation time: 5 minutes
Cooking time: about 20 minutes

4–6 cups (1–1 1/2 l) water
5 to 6 lb. (2–3 kg) lutefisk
(1 1/2 tablespoons salt)

1. Bring the water to the boil and add the pieces of fish.
   NOTE: do not cook the lutefisk in an aluminium saucepan, any residual lye will corrode the aluminium. Pour off the cooking liquid. Serve in the same way as for baked lutefisk.

Hint
The pieces of fish will retain their shape if they are boiled tied up in a cheesecloth.

White sauce
Preparation time: 5–10 minutes
Cooking time: about 10 minutes

5 tablespoons margarine
3/4 cups (2 dl) white flour
6 cups (1 1/2 l) milk
salt to taste

1. Melt the margarine in a saucepan, add the flour and stir well
2. Add the milk gradually while stirring and allow to boil gently for about 10 minutes.
3. Season with salt. When ready the sauce should be smooth and shiny.

Cranberry parfait
Preparation time: 40 minutes
Freezing time: 4–5 hours or overnight.

1/2 cup (1 1/2 dl) water and
1/2 cup (1 1/2 dl) sugar, or
1 cup (3 dl) fruit juice
6 egg yolks
2 1/2 cups (6 dl) whipping cream
1 1/2 liters frozen cranberries (or cloudberries, lingonberries or blackcurrants)
cranberries for decorating

1. Bring the sugar and water, or fruit juice, to the boil.
2. Beat the egg yolks in a bowl and add the boiling sugar water or fruit juice, beating vigorously all the time.
3. Pour into a saucepan and continue to beat over a low heat until it thickens. Do not let it boil.
4. Allow to cool, for instance by placing the saucepan in a bowl of cold water. Beat occasionally.
5. Whip up the cream and fold into the cooled mixture.
6. Add the mashed berries.
7. Transfer the mixture to a deep mold or bowl which has been rinsed with cold water, and freeze.
8. Remove the parfait from the mold by dipping for a moment in hot water. Invert onto a serving dish and decorate with the whole cranberries.

Hint
Parfait can be made in a quicker and easier way as follows: beat six whole eggs with the sugar, and the cream separately. Combine the whipped egg mixture and whipped cream, and flavour with berry purée or fruit. Add sugar according to taste. Pour into a glass or stoneware serving bowl and freeze. Remove from the freezer half an hour before serving. Decorate with whipped cream and berries.

New Year's Eve

The old time furniture and log walls blend in to give a special atmosphere for this New Year's Eve meal. For a starter, elk or a regular meat soup will be the first course and is served from a big game pot. The midnight meal, except the baked potatoes, may be prepared the day before.

New Year's eve supper
(for 10 persons)

Finnish elk soup
Apple pie
Vanilla custard
Coffee

Midnight snack
(for 10 persons)

Roast beef
Baked potatoes
Relishes and pickles
Pickled beets

Finnish elk soup

Preparation time: about 30 minutes
Cooking time: about 2 1/2 hours

3 1/4 lb. (1 1/2 kg) frozen shoulder, rib or breast of elk (or venison)
20 cups (5 l) water
2 tablespoons salt
20 whole allspice
3 onions
2 leeks
1 parsnip
half a celery
(1/3 cup (1 dl) pearl barley)
8 cups (2 l) potatoes
bunch of parsley

1. Put the meat, while still frozen, into cold water and bring to the boil. Remove any foam which is formed.
2. Add the seasoning and spices (and the barley) and continue to boil for at least an hour. Add the chopped up vegetables, but not the potatoes.
3. Remove the meat when it is tender and add the peeled potatoes to the soup.
4. Remove all the meat from the bones and cut up into small chunks. Return to the almost ready soup.
5. Check the seasoning and add the finely-chopped tops of the leeks or parsley and serve while piping hot.

Apple pie

Preparing the pastry: 15 minutes
Preparing the filling: 30–40 minutes
Baking time: about 1 hour
Oven temperature: 350 °F (180 °C)
Suitable for freezing

Pastry: 5 oz. (150 g) margarine or butter
5 oz. (150 g) white flour (about 2 1/2 dl)
1/4 cup (1/2 dl) water
Filling: about 3 cups (700 g) tart apples
1/3 cup (1 dl) sugar
1 teaspoon ground cinnamon
1–2 tablespoons butter
(1–2 tablespoons honey)

1. Cut in the margarine and flour together, add the water and mix. Do not knead, otherwise the pastry will become tough.
2. Leave to rest for a short time in a cool place.
3. Peel and slice the apples.
4. Roll out 2/3 of the pastry and use it to line the bottom and edges of the dish, leaving a strip an inch wide overlapping the edges.
5. Put the apple slices, sugar and cinnamon in layers in the dish. Dot with a few pats of butter and, if desired, add the honey. In this case use less sugar.
6. Turn the overhanging edges of the pastry back over the top of the filling and brush them with cold water.
7. Roll out the rest of the pastry, place over the pie and seal the edges.
8. Prick the top in a few places with a fork to allow the steam to escape.
9. Bake in the oven for about one hour and serve hot in the same dish with vanilla sauce or ice cream.

Vanilla custard

Preparation time: 15 minutes
Cooking time: 20 minutes
Not suitable for freezing

4 egg yolks
4 tablespoons sugar
4 tablespoons potato starch
2 1/2 cups (6 dl) milk
1 teaspoons vanilla extract
3/4 cup (2 dl) cream

1. Mix all the ingredients, except the vanilla extract and cream, in a saucepan.
2. Place over a low heat and stir continuously until the custard thickens.
3. Allow to cool, stirring occasionally.
4. Flavour with the vanilla extract and fold in the thickly-whipped cream.

NOTE: If you make the custard in an aluminium saucepan, use a wooden or plastic utensil. A stainless steel whisk will remove a little aluminium from the pan and turn the custard grey.

Roast beef

Preparation time: 5 minutes
Cooking time: 1 1/2–2 hours
Oven temperature: 300–350 °F (150–175 °C)

about 5 lb. (2 kg) joint of prime beef
1 1/2 tablespoons salt
1 teaspoon white pepper

1. Put the beef on a wire rack in a roasting pan with the fatty side up.
2. Push a roasting thermometer into the thickest part of the joint being careful not to let it touch the bone.
3. Roast until the reading is about 145 °F (60–65 °C). The centre of the joint will then be a beautiful pink colour. If you would like the joint to be medium done in the middle, wait until the reading is as high as 160 °F (72 °C).

4. Let the meat stand for about 10 minutes.

5. Carve the joint across the grain into thin slices and sprinkle a little salt and pepper on each slice.

Different types of pickled relishes — pumpkin pickle, vegetable pickle and Grandma's cucumber salad (see p. 36), grated horseradish, tart jams or jellies all go very well with roast beef. A juicy roast does not need any gravy or sauces.

Hint 1
It is important to use a low oven temperature when roasting beef in the oven, the meat will be juicier and the weight loss smaller than with a higher temperature. However, with a roasting temperature of, for instance, 212 °F (100 °C) the roasting time will be 5–6 hours.

Hint 2
If you want to give the roast a uni-

form and delicate flavour of garlic, push three sliced cloves of garlic into the roast the previous evening.

Baked potatoes
Preparation time: 15 minutes
Cooking time: about 1 hour
Oven temperature: 385 °F (200 °C)

1 large or 2 small potatoes per person
butter

1. Scrub the even-sized potatoes well with a stiff brush.

2. Pour a little oil into the palm of your hand and rub the potatoes with it. This will give them a crispy skin.

3. Wrap each potato in aluminium foil and bake in the oven. Medium-sized potatoes will take about 50–60 minutes.

4. Make two cross-wise incisions in the top of each potato, squeeze

An old cupboard acts as an ideal side table for the coffee and tea cups (above).

The narrow table cloth accentuates the beautiful turquoise of the table. Dark plates and oven-proof serving dishes and the cobolt-blue roaster complement the color scheme. Silver is a color for the New Year's table — the baked potatoes are wrapped in aluminium foil (on the right).

gently to make the tops open and add a good dab of butter.

Hint
The butter can also be flavoured with garlic or chives, or else replaced by plain or flavoured sour cream.

Lent

Lent in Finland is traditionally a time for outdoor parties. Everybody lends a hand to build a toboggan slide where children and adults alike have tremendous fun. Lanterns and candles are hung in the surrounding trees. Such parties require food which can be made beforehand and is ready to warm up when everybody comes back to the house afterwards. Pigs feet, pea soup and Lenten buns are ideal for this.

Lenten supper
(for 10 persons)

Pigs' feet
Pea soup

Lenten buns
Hot chocolate

Pigs' feet
Preparation time: 10 minutes
Cooking time: 2 1/2–3 hours
Suitable for freezing

about 4 1/2 lb. (2 kg) pig's feet, preferably forelegs
12 cups (3 l) water
3 tablespoons salt
15 white peppercorns
2 bay leaves

1. Rinse the feet with cold water and then place in cold water in a saucepan. Bring to a boil, remove any foam and then add the seasoning.
2. Cook over a low heat until tender. Test with a toothpick.
3. Allow to cool and serve prior to the pea soup.

Hint
Pig's feet are also excellent for an evening snack with bread and butter and pickled beets. They are easiest to eat with your fingers, so keep plenty of paper napkins available. The cooking liquid can be used as a stock for soups.

Pea soup
Preparation time: 10 minutes
Cooking time: about 2 1/2 hours
Soaking time for peas: overnight
Suitable for freezing

3 3/4 cups (9 dl) whole or split dry green peas
20 cups (5 l) water
2 1/4 lb. (1 kg) pork and leg of pork
2 tablespoons salt
2 onions
(marjoram)
mustard

1. Wash the peas and soak overnight in slightly-salted cold water.
2. Boil the peas in the same liquid and add the finley-chopped onions.
3. Add the pork when the peas are partly cooked.
4. Simmer gently until the peas and meat are thoroughly cooked.
5. Remove the meat from the bones, cut up into small pieces and return to the soup.

6. Add some water if necessary to obtain the desired consistency. Season, if desired, with finely-chopped marjoram just before serving.
7. Serve mustard on the table so that everyone can season their own soup.

Hint
Pea soup can be prepared in half the time using a pressure cooker. If you have a freezer it is worth making pea soup in bulk and freezing part of it.

Lenten buns and hot chocolate
(makes 10 buns)
Preparation time: 15 minutes
Make the buns from the dough for sweet bread ring (see p. 48);
use half the amount.
The buns are suitable for freezing

Filling: 1 1/4 cups (3 dl) cream
1 tablespoon sugar
Hot chocolate:
6 cups (1 1/2 l) milk
4 tablespoons cocoa powder
2 tablespoons sugar

1. Whip up the cream and sugar for the filling.
2. Split the buns and fill with the whipped cream.
3. Bring the milk to the boil. Mix the cocoa and sugar together and add to the hot milk, stirring vigorously.
4. Put a bun in each dessert bowl and pour over the hot chocolate just before serving.

Lent buns are served in the traditional way with hot chocolate (on the left).

The table for a Lenten party is as simple as possible. A linen, handwoven sauna towel makes an ideal table cloth. The pig's feet and tureen of pea soup are rushed to the table and everybody is ready to tuck in. Dried grass from summer makes a perfect decoration (on the right).

Easter

Lamb or mutton is traditionally served for Easter dinner. Roast lamb makes an easy meal and is just as good when served cold. Easter Pasha, which has been introduced from the East and has become a permanent fixture of Easter in Finland, is served with the coffee.

Easter dinner
(for 10 persons)

Cream of spinach soup

Roast lamb
Garlic potatoes
Carrot and pickle salad
Grandma's cucumber salad

Fruit savarin

Easter coffee table
(for 10 persons)

Coffee
Easter pasha
Dripperpan sweet bread

Cream of spinach soup
Preparation time: 5–10 minutes
Cooking time: about 20 minutes
Suitable for freezing

Rich, heavy food is served for Easter dinner. A multicolored, linen table cloth artfully repeats the colors of the food, from the painted eggs to the grated carrot and fruit savarin. The joining colour, lilac, can be seen in the candles, napkins, eggs, stripes of the table cloth, savarin dish and even in the refreshment. One-colored dishes are essential with such multicolored fare. Pussy willows make an attractive center-piece.

33

3 tablespoons margarine
5–6 tablespoons white flour
8 cups (2 l) milk or meat stock
1 1/4 cups (300 g) frozen spinach
salt to taste
a little sugar

1. Melt the margarine in a saucepan and add the flour. Bring to the boil and simmer gently for a few minutes, but do not let it brown.
2. Add the milk or stock and the frozen chopped spinach.
3. Simmer for about 15 minutes and season with salt and a little sugar.

Hint

If you want to make a richer soup, beat two egg yolks and 1/2 cup (1 dl) cream in a bowl and slowly stir into the soup.

Roast lamb

Roast lamb is an easy meal to prepare for Easter dinner, it cooks by itself in the oven. The hostess then has time to entertain the guests. Roast lamb is also very tasty when served cold.

Preparation time: about 15 minutes
Cooking time: 2–2 1/2 hours
Oven temperature: 350 °F (175 °C)
Suitable for freezing

5 to 6 lb. (2 1/2–3 kg) joint of lamb
3–5 cloves of garlic
white pepper
salt
rosemary
3 tablespoons butter

1. Make a few cuts in the surface of the meat and push in the sliced garlic cloves, preferably the previous evening.
2. Rub the white pepper, salt and rosemary over the surface of the joint and add a few pats of butter.
3. Push the roasting thermometer into the thickest part of the joint, but not right against the bone.
4. Put the joint on a wire rack and

A leg of lamb roasted in a medium oven makes a tasty party meal (on the left).

The fruit savarin is served for dessert in a wide, shallow dish, Easter Pasha belongs on the coffee and tea table.

place in the oven above a roasting tin which can be used for cooking the garlic potatoes.

5. Remove the roast from the oven when the roasting thermometer reads 170 °F (75–80 °C). The joint will be rare in the middle if it is removed at 160 °F (72 °C). Let the roast stand for about 10 minutes before carving.

Garlic potatoes
Preparation time: 30 minutes
Cooking time: 2–2 1/2 hours
Oven temperature: 350 °F (175 °C)

4 lb. (2 kg) potatoes
3 1/2 oz. (100 g) butter
1 tablespoon salt
3–5 garlic cloves

1. Peel the potatoes and cut into thick slices.
2. Melt the butter in the roasting tin and add the potato slices, salt and crushed cloves of garlic. Toss the potatoes in the mixture.
2. Place the roasting tin under the leg of lamb (see previous recipe). Leave to cook slowly under the roast, the juices from the meat will baste the potatoes.

Carrot and pickle salad
Preparation time: 15 minutes

6 medium-sized carrots
1 small jar of sweet relish or pickle

Scrub and peel the carrots. Grate and mix with the relish.

Grandma's cucumber salad
Preparation time: 10 minutes
Marinading time: 15 minutes

1 large cucumber
1/4 cup (1/2 dl) sugar
1 teaspoon salt
some fresh dill
1 lb. (1/4 dl) vinegar
1/4 cup (1/2 dl) water

1. Slice the cucumber into a container with a lid.
2. Cover the cucumber with the sugar, salt and finely-chopped dill.
3. Put the lid on tightly and shake vigorously for a couple of minutes or until the sugar has dissolved.

Leave to marinade. Add the vinegar and water to taste.
4. Empty into a serving bowl and garnish with dill.

Fruit savarin
Preparation time: 20 minutes
Rising time: 1–1 1/2 hours
Cooking time: 30 minutes
Oven temperature: 400 °F (200 °C)
Not suitable for freezing

1/2 cup (1 1/2 dl) milk
3 tablespoons sugar
1/2 teaspoon salt
1 teaspoon vanilla sugar or extract
about 20 g yeast or 1 pkg dry yeast
2 eggs
2 oz. (50 g) butter or margarine
1 1/2 cups (250 g) white flour (about 4 dl)
For moistening: 1 cup (2 1/2 dl) apple or pear juice, or fresh orange juice with a dash of lemon juice.
Filling: fruit or berries

1. Grease a cake mold or cake pan.
2. Heat the milk to hand temperature and add the sugar, salt and vanilla. Crumble the yeast into the milk and mix well.
3. Beat the eggs until light and add to the milk mixture. Follow with the flour and melted butter or margarine.
4. Pour into the cake tin and allow to rise in a warm place until double in bulk.
5. Bake in the oven for half an hour and test when done with a toothpick.
6. Moisten the cake in the cake tin with juice while still warm. It will absorb the juice more thoroughly.
7. Leave to stand in a cool place for a couple of hours, preferably overnight.
8. Invert the cake tin onto a serving dish. Fill the centre with berries or fruit.

Easter pasha
Preparation time: about 40 minutes
Cooling and setting time: 1 day

1 cup (200 g) butter
1/3 to 1/2 cup (1–1 1/2 dl) sugar
3/4 cup (2 dl) whipping cream
1 lb. (500 g) cottage cheese

2 eggs yolks
2 teaspoons vanilla extract
2 tablespoons lemon juice
2 tablespoons finely-chopped almonds
1/3 cup (1 dl) candied peel (candied cherries)

1. Cream the butter and sugar together, whip up the cream.
2. Mix both together with the creamed cottage cheese and egg yolks. Add the other ingredients and blend the mixture well.
3. Transfer to a cheesecloth and leave to drain in a cheese mold or other suitable receptacle, such as a colander, coffee strainer or flower pot.
4. Press the mixture down well and place a weight on top.
5. Place the mold in another container since rather a lot of liquid will drain out of the pasha.
6. Keep overnight in the refrigerator and invert before serving onto a serving dish.

Sweet bread in a dripperpan
Preparation time: 20 minutes
Rising time: 40 minutes
Cooking time: 40–50 minutes
Oven temperature: 350 °F (175 °C)
Suitable for freezing

2 eggs
3/4 cup (2 dl) sugar
1 1/4 cups (3 dl) milk
2 teaspoons salt
3 teaspoons crushed cardamom seeds
about 40 g yeast or 2 pkgs dry yeast
2/3 cup (150 g) margarine
about 1 1/2 cups (350 g) white flour (5 1/2 dl)
sliced almonds for decoration

1. Grease a dripperpan (9 × 13 inches).
2. Whip up the eggs and sugar and mix in the lukewarm milk, spices, crumbled yeast, melted margarine and flour. Mix well.
3. Pour the mixture into the pan and allow to rise.
4. Brush the top with egg and decorate with sliced almonds. Bake in the oven until golden brown.

Christenings

Christenings in Finland are very often held at home. The food which is served is simple but stylish. Cheese-filled cream puffs make a tasty morsel, accompanied by sweet bread rings, wafer-thin almond snaps and rosy dream role.

Christening party
(for 15 persons)

Cheese-filled cream puffs
Sweet bread rings
Almond snaps
Rosy dream roll
Coffee

Cheese-filled cream puffs

(makes about 40)
Preparation time: 30 minutes + 15 minutes
Baking time: 30 minutes/batch
Oven temperature: 350 °F (175 °C)
Suitable for freezing without the filling

1 1/2 cups (4 dl) water
2/3 cup (150 g) butter
2/3 cup (150 g) white flour (about 2 1/2 dl)
4 eggs
Filling: 1/3 cup (1 dl) cream
7 oz. (200 g) blue cheese
1 grated apple

1. Boil up the water and butter in a saucepan. Add the flour, mixing well, and continue to cook until the dough separates from the sides of the pan.
2. Add the eggs one at a time when the mixture has cooled a little and whip up vigorously.
3. Shape smallish balls from the mixture using two spoons and place on the baking tray.
4. Bake in the oven for about 30 minutes. Do not open the oven door during the first 15 minutes or otherwise they will collapse.
5. Whip up the cream and mix in the grated apple and blue cheese. Cut each puff ball in half, fill the bottom half with the mixture and replace the lid.

Hint
The puff balls can be made a few days before and filled just before serving.

Sweet bread rings

(makes about 35)
Preparation time: 30 minutes
Rising time: about 1 hour
Baking time: about 7 minutes/batch
Oven temperature: 440 °F (225 °C)
Suitable for freezing

2 eggs
1/2 cup (1 1/2 dl) sugar
1 1/4 cups (3 dl) milk
1 teaspoon salt
2 teaspoons cardamom seeds
2 tablespoons yeast
2/3 cup (150 g) margarine
2 1/3 cups (550 g) white flour (about 9 dl)
Egg for glazing
Pearl sugar for decorating

1. Crush the cardamom seeds and warm up the milk to hand warm.
2. Whip up the eggs and sugar.
3. Mix in the warm milk, yeast, spices and flour in small portions.
4. Mix the dough and then add the margarine which has warmed up to room temperature.
5. Roll out small pieces of partly-risen dough into thin ropes. Wind the ends around each other to form rings.
6. Leave the rings to rise. Brush with egg and sprinkle with pearl sugar. Bake in the oven.

A white christening bowl, white table cloth and white Holy Bible dominate the christening table.

Almond snaps

(makes about 40)
Preparation time: about 30 minutes
Baking time: about 7 minutes/batch
Oven temperature: 300 °F (150 °C)
Not suitable for freezing

3 1/2 oz. (100 g) margarine
1/3 cup (1 dl) sugar
3 1/2 oz. (100 g) blanched almonds
2 tablespoons milk
3 tablespoons white flour

1. Grind up the almonds.
2. Measure out all the ingredients into a saucepan and bring to a boil.
3. Put teaspoons of the mixture onto a cookie sheet, sprinkled with potato or corn starch.
4. Bake the snaps until golden brown.
5. If you want curved snaps, roll around a rolling pin while still warm. Store in a dry place.

Alternative
Oat snaps are easier, cheaper and quicker to make.

Pink roses accentuate the simple perfection of the cake.

Oat snaps

(makes about 40)
Preparation time: about 10 minutes
Baking time: about 10 minutes
Oven temperature: 300 °F (150 °C)
Not suitable for freezing

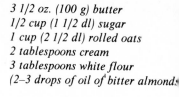

3 1/2 oz. (100 g) butter
1/2 cup (1 1/2 dl) sugar
1 cup (2 1/2 dl) rolled oats
2 tablespoons cream
3 tablespoons white flour
(2–3 drops of oil of bitter almonds)

1. Melt the butter and mix in all
the other ingredients.
2. Cover a cookie sheet with evenly
spaced dollops of the mixture.
Bake in the oven until golden
brown.
3. Remove when still warm from
the cookie sheet using a spatula and
roll around a bottle to make them
curved.

Rosy dream roll

Preparation time: about 30 minutes
Baking time: 10–15 minutes
Suitable for freezing

*Sponge cake mixture (see cloudber-
ry cake, p. 50)
Filling: 4 cups (1 l) lingonberries or
2 cups (1/2 l) lingonberry purée
3/4 cup (2 dl) whipping cream
1/3 cup (1 dl) sugar
Coating: 1 1/2 cups (4 dl) whipping
cream
2 tablespoons sugar
(juice from half a lemon)*

1. Line a jelly roll pan with wax
paper. Prepare the sponge cake
mixture and pour into the pan.
2. Spread out evenly with a spatula
and bake in the oven.
3. Sprinkle with sugar and invert
onto paper.
4. Whip up the cream and flavor
with sugar and lingonberry purée.
Spread over the cake when cool and
roll up to form a jelly roll.
5. Add the sugar (and the lemon
juice) to the cream and whip up.
Spread over the jelly roll.

*Carefully-chosen cookies and deli-
cate colors make a suitable table
setting for the occasion. The pink
ribbons on the living, naturally
colored tablecloth are a thoughtful
touch. The napkins, candles and
flowers are the same shade as the
ribbons. White dishes go well
together with the intimate, light
atmosphere.*

Children's Birthday Parties

Children's parties are best planned and prepared together with the children. They learn how to plan parties and become used to helping mother in the kitchen right from the start. The food should be attractive and well-balanced. As well as sweet dishes, different types of vegetables, fruit and something savoury is also served.

Children's party
(for 10 children)

Cheese tray
Apple juice

Raisin dough boys
Hot chocolate and whipped cream

Ice cream train

Cheese tray
Preparation time: 20 minutes

3 or 4 different types of mild cheese
red peppers
carrots
apples or pears
ginger cookies or snaps

Cut up the cheese into cubes and the fruit and vegetables into manageable pieces and arrange on a tray together with the ginger cookies. Serve with refreshing apple juice.

Raisin dough boys
Preparation time: 20 minutes
Baking time: about 15 minutes
Suitable for freezing

Make half a litre of sweet bread (see dough p. 48) and fashion into boy shapes. Decorate with raisins when the dough has risen.

Hot chocolate and whipped cream
Preparation time: 15 minutes

6 cups (1 1/2 l) milk
1/3 cup (1 dl) cocoa
1/3 cup (1 dl) sugar
Topping: 1/2 cup (1 1/2 dl) cream
2 teaspoons sugar
chocolate flakes

1. Boil up the milk and beat in the cocoa and sugar mixture.
2. Portion out the hot chocolate and top with whipped cream and chocolate flakes.

Hint
You can prepare a richer chocolate drink by first boiling the cocoa in water for a few minutes and then adding the milk and sugar and heating the mixture.

Ice cream train
Select a number of different types and packet sizes of ice cream. Construct a train out of the ice cream and decorate with pieces of chocolate and sweets.

Children should be taught right
from the start how to make attractive table settings. A blue, plastic-
coated cloth protects the table. The
serving and eating dishes are sturdy
glass and enamelware (above).

The highlight of the children's party is the candle-studded birthday
cake — in this case an ice-cream
train formed from standard packs
of strawberry, vanilla and chocolate ice-cream. The smokestack is
an ice-cream stick topped with
whipped cream, the buffers and
wheels of liquorice and the wagons
loaded with sweets (on the left).

Graduation Party

School is over, summer is ahead and it's time to celebrate graduation. Relatives, friends and acquaintances come and go in a steady stream. The buffet on offer is like a fresh breath of spring. The weather determines where the food and refreshment will be served — in the garden or on the terrace if it is sunny and warm. Planning for the party started the previous summer with the canning or freezing of the berries to be served.

Toast to spring
(for 20 persons)

Spring punch

Open-faced ham sandwiches
Open-faced mushroom salad sandwiches

Spice cake
Ice cream and berries
Caramel sauce
Coffee

Spring punch
Punch, made from homemade fruit juice and fizzy drinks, is served for drinking a toast.

A well-smoothed, plain tablecloth shows highly-prized dishes and cutlery at their best. Colorful, open faced sandwiches served on a one-color ceramic dish, punch, fresh berries and the dinner service bring so much life to the table that if any flowers are used they should be subdued (on the left).

8 cups (2 l) apple juice or other fruit juice
4 bottles of soda water
slices of lemon and cucumber
ice cubes

Mix just before serving and garnish with thin slices of lemon and cucumber.

Alternative
Homemade mead is ideally suited as a base for punch.

Mead
Preparation time: 15 minutes
Fermentation time: 3–6 days

32 cups (8 l) water
2 1/2 lb. (1 kg) brown sugar
2 lemons
1/4 teaspoon yeast
1 dl dark karo syrup

1. Carefully wash the lemons and pare off the yellow skin with, for instance, a potato peeler.
2. Put the lemon peel and sugar in the bottom of a large container. Boil up half of the water and pour over the sugar and lemon peel.
3. Remove the white layer of peel from around the lemons and cut them up into slices. Add to the mixture and finish filling with the rest of the cold water.
4. Allow to cool down to hand warm and add the yeast.
5. Keep at room temperature and ferment until the following day.
6. Put a few raisins and a teaspoon of sugar in a number of clean bottles. Strain the mead into the bottles.
7. Screw the bottle caps on loosely and store in a cool place. The mead is ready to drink when the raisins rise to the top.

Hint 1
If you want to speed up the process, keep the bottles at room temperature for one day and then in the cool for one or two days.

Hint 2
If you want a lighter colored drink, substitute half of the brown sugar with ordinary sugar; the amount of sugar can also be reduced by one third.

Open-faced ham and mushroom salad sandwiches

2 rye bread loaves, baked in tins
mashed potatoes
mushroom salad
sliced ham
Garnishing: green part of a leek
cucumber
lettuce leaves
(apples
prunes)

First of all prepare the filling for the sandwiches. Buttery mashed potatoes can be used instead of butter.

Buttery mashed potatoes
Preparation time: about 30 minutes
Cooking time: about 20 minutes

1 1/4 cups (300 g) peeled potatoes

1 1/4 cups (300 g) butter
salt to taste

1. Boil the peeled potatoes in a little water until soft.
2. Mash the potatoes, season with salt, cool and then add the softened butter. This will give a very creamy mixture.

Mushroom salad
Preparation time: about 20 minutes

about 1 1/2 lb. (750 g) frozen or salted wild mushrooms
1 small leek
3/4 cup (2 dl) whipping cream
white pepper
(salt)

1. Chop up the mushrooms finely; remove excess salt from the salted

mushrooms by soaking in cold water.
2. Finely slice the leek and whip up the cream.
3. Mix all the ingredients together and season with pepper and, if necessary, sea salt.

Open-faced sandwiches
Preparation time: about 1 1/2 hours

1. Remove the top and bottom crusts from the loaves and cut up lengthwise into centimeter-thick slices.
2. Spread with the mashed potatoes and cut the slices into the desired shapes.
3. Cover with lettuce. Add mushroom salad to half of the sandwiches and ham to the other half.

44

Garnish the mushroom sandwiches with leek rings and the ham sandwiches with cucumber slices. Apple and prunes also go very well with ham.

NOTE: Bread which is one-day-old is the best because it does not crumble and is otherwise easy to handle and cut up. Sandwiches for a buffet should be small, about 5 × 5 cm. Reserve 3–4 sandwiches for each quest depending on what else is served. A medium-sized loaf will make about 30 sandwiches.

Spice cake
Preparation time: 20 minutes
Baking time: 50–60 minutes
Oven temperature: 340 °F (170 °C)
Suitable for freezing

2 eggs
1 3/4 cups (400 g) brown sugar (about 5 dl)
1 teaspoon ground cinnamon
1 teaspoon ground cloves
2 teaspoons crushed cardamom
1 1/2 cups (100 g) margarine
3/4 cup (2 dl) thick sour cream
1 1/4 cups (about 300 g) white flour (4 1/2 dl)
1 1/2 teaspoons bicarbonate of soda
1/3 cup (1 dl) raisins or other chopped dried fruit

1. Grease a cake mould and dust with rolled or sliced almonds.
2. Melt the margarine. Beat up the eggs and brown sugar until fluffy and add the margarine. Mix in the spices, sour cream, flour and soda mixture and chopped-up raisins.
3. Do not beat the mixture. Pour into the cake mould and bake in the oven until golden brown.
4. Do not remove the cake from the mould straight after taking it out of the oven, let it cool for a short time.

Spice cake is always successful and keeps well.

Ice cream and berries
16 cups (4 l) vanilla ice cream
8–12 cups (2–3 l) berries

Serve caramel sauce with the ice cream and berries.

Caramel sauce
Preparation time: about 40 minutes

1 1/2 cups (4 dl) sugar
3/4 cup (2 dl) water
2 cups (5 dl) whipping cream
1 teaspoon vanilla sugar or extract

1. Melt the sugar in a hot frying pan. Check that the sugar melts evenly. Stir all the time and let the sugar brown a little, but be careful it does not burn.
2. Add the boiling water and simmer over a low heat until it is an even consistency.
3. Boil up the cream in a saucepan and add the sugar mixture.
4. Boil gently for about 20 minutes until it starts to thicken a little.

House-warming Party

Friends, acquaintances and even the new neighbors, are invited to house-warming parties. The menu has been planned with economy in mind. A modern variation on the traditional Finnish dish — Fish in a crust — is served as the main course. A delicious cheesecake makes an easy and quick dessert.

Old recipes in a new way
(for 20 persons)

Cranberry tea

Fish in a crust
Beet and onion salad

Cheesecake
Berries or jam
Tea or coffee

Cranberry tea
Preparation time: 15 minutes

2 1/4 lb. (1 kg) cranberries
2 1/2 cups (6 dl) sugar
10 cups (2 1/2 l) strong tea
3/4 cup (2 dl) whipping cream for topping

1. Mash the cranberries with the sugar and pour over the boiling tea.
2. Leave to cool and strain into chilled glasses.
3. The drink can be topped with a dollop of whipped cream. Serve as cold as possible.

Fish in a crust
Cleaning the fish: about 1 hour
Preparation time: about 45 minutes
Baking time: 2–2 1/2 hours
Oven temperature: 325 °F (160 °C)

2 large sour rye loaves
6 1/2 lb. (3 kg) vendace or other small fish

1 lb. (800 g) side of fresh pork or bacon
4 onions
6 teaspoons salt

1. Clean the fish. It is best to do this by pulling out the gills and gut without opening the belly skin. Quickly rinse under cold water and leave to drain.
2. Brown the sliced pork and onions.
3. Slice off the top of the loaves and scoop out the contents with a spoon.
4. Fill the hollowed-out loaves with alternate layers of meat and onions, and fish. Season each layer of fish with salt. When they are filled completely replace the lids. The surface of the loaves can be brushed lightly with butter or margarine.
5. Wrap up tightly in aluminium foil and bake in the oven.

Hint
The insides of the bread can be used to make a sour bread pudding. Unless you think it would be too rich, this pudding could be served as dessert after the fish in a crust.

Sour bread pudding
Drying the breadcrumbs: about 20 minutes
Preparation time: 20 minutes
Cooking time: 30–40 minutes
Oven temperature: 325 °F (160 °C)

fresh breadcrumbs
rhubarb, apple or lingonberry purée
butter or margarine

1. Dry and lightly brown the breadcrumbs in the oven at the same time as the fish in a crust.
2. Grease a baking dish and fill with alternate layers of the bread crumbs and fruit purée.
3. Dot the top with butter and margarine and bake in the oven.
Serve it hot with ice cream, vanilla custard or a mixture of milk and cream.

Beet and onion salad
Preparation time: 20 minutes
Not suitable for freezing

3 lb. (1 1/2 kg) pickled boiled beets
6 onions
a little sugar
a dash of salt
onion or leek for decorating

1. Buy the beets ready pickled. Grate the beets roughly. Do the same with the onions, mix together with the beets and add salt and sugar to taste.
2. Toss the mixture lightly using two forks. Garnish with onion or leek rings.

Cheesecake
(for 10 persons)
Preparation time: 10 minutes
Baking time: 30–40 minutes
Oven temperature: 350 °F (175 °C)
Not suitable for freezing

1 1/2 cups (4 dl) cottage cheese
1 1/2 cups (4 dl) thick sour cream
5 eggs
2 tablespoons sugar
2 teaspoons vanilla sugar or extract
fresh berries or jam

1. Mix all the ingredients together in a blender (except the berries or jam) and pour into one large, or two small, greased oven-safe platters or serving dishes.
2. Bake in the oven and serve hot or cold with the berries or jam.

The green-chequered cotton table-cloth is in the same shade as the greyish set of dishes. The fish in a crust is easy to cut on a thick wooden board. A narrow desk is used as the buffet table, but the stainless steel draining board in the kitchen would be just as good.

Anniversaries

Father's fiftieth birthday and successive ten-year anniversaries are important occasions in Finnish society. An announcement in the local newspaper, which does not include a note to say that the family will be away, is sufficient to indicate that all visitors will be welcome at the house. Such important occasions are planned very carefully weeks ahead. A homemade sweet bread ring and fancy filled cake are always offered. Two or three types of cookies are usually also served. The coffee table should also include something savory.

Anniversary coffee table
(for 10 persons)

Champagne or cider
Sweet bread ring
Cloudberry cream cake
Cinnamon S cookies
Barley cookies
Flat cheese (see p. 60)
Rye bread rolls
Coffee

Sweet bread ring
Preparation time: 30 minutes
Rising time: 1 1/2 + 1 1/2 hours
Baking time: about 30 minutes
Oven temperature: 400 °F (200 °C)
Suitable for freezing

2 eggs
3/4 cup (2 dl) sugar
2 cups (1/2 l) milk
50 g yeast or 2 pkgs dry yeast
3 teaspoons salt
1 tablespoon crushed cardamom
1/2 lb. (250 g) butter or margarine
or 3/4 cup (2 dl) cooking oil
about 2 1/4 lb. (1 kg) white flour
(15–16 dl)

1/3 cup (1 dl) raisins
egg yolk for glazing
almonds for decorating

1. Put the ingredients for the dough ready in the kitchen the previous evening. If they are cold the dough will take too long to rise.
2. Heat the milk to hand temperature so as to enhance the action of the yeast.
3. Beat up the eggs and sugar, add the milk, yeast, salt and cardamom. If oil is to be used, add it at this stage.
4. Add enough of the flour to give a thick, elastic mixture. Beat it vigorously to put air into the dough. This will enhance the glutination of the flour and make the dough rise well.
5. Mix in the rest of the flour and finally the butter or margarine. Knead the dough until it separates completely from your hands and sides of the bowl. Add the raisins just before shaping the ring.
6. If you make the dough with an electric dough mixer, follow closely the instructions for preparing dough.
7. Cover the dough with a cloth and leave to rise in a warm place. When the dough has doubled in bulk, place on a lightly floured surface and knead well. Add the raisins.
8. Form the ring by braiding together three or four strands of dough. If you think it is too difficult to make a ring like this, form in two or three separate curved sections and place on a baking tray to

The table setting has been planned to fit in with the color scheme of the home — in this case light shades. A natural-colored, coarse-linen tablecloth is ideal for the occasion and goes perfectly with the coffee cups which are decorated with cloth-colored, black and beige stripes. Tea cups are set on the table because there are always some tea drinkers among a large group of guests. If different type of cups have to be used, they should be grouped separately. An anniversary gift of a flower vase and white roses have the place of honor.

rise. The ring can then be assembled on the serving dish after baking.

9. Cover the ring with a cloth and leave to rise in a warm place. The dough has risen enough if, after pressing a finger lightly into the dough, the depression disappears.

10. Brushing the ring with egg yolk will give it a beautiful colour and finish when baked. Sprinkle with crushed or sliced almonds. Bake in the oven for about half an hour.

11. If you intend to freeze the ring, do it as soon as it has cooled down properly.

Cloudberry cream cake
(3–4 cakes for 50 people)
Preparation time: 30 minutes
Baking time: 30–40 minutes
Oven temperature: 350–400 °F (180–200 °C)
Suitable for freezing

Sponge cake:
6 eggs
1 1/4 cups (3 dl) sugar
2/3 cup (1 1/2 dl) white flour
2/3 cup (1 1/2 dl) potato flour
1 1/2 teaspoons baking powder
Soaking: juice of one lemon
1 tablespoon sugar
1/3 cup (1 dl) water
Filling: 2 cups (5 dl) cloudberries or raspberries
1 1/4 cups (3 dl) whipping cream
1/3 cup (1 dl) sugar
Coating: 2 cups (5 dl) whipping cream
4–5 tablespoons sugar
juice of half a lemon
cloudberries for decorating.

1. Grease a large cake tin and coat with dried breadcrumbs.

2. Beat up the eggs and sugar until fluffy. Mix the baking powder with the flour and gradually add to the egg mixture.

3. Bake in the oven and leave to cool. Split the cake into three unequal layers, the bottom one should be the thickest and the top one the thinnest.

4. Moisten the cake with the sweetened, diluted lemon juice. Spread the cloudberries and sweetened whipped cream between the layers, preferably the previous evening so that the cake will be evenly moistened.

5. Whip up the cream, sugar and lemon juice and spread evenly over the cake. Decorate with cloudberries. (Raspberries can be used instead).

Cinnamon S cookies
(makes about 60)
Preparation time: 20 minutes
Resting time for the dough: 1–2 hours

aking time: about 10 minutes/
atch
oven temperature: 340 °F (170 °C)
hese keep well

/2 cup (100 g) butter or margarine
/4 cup (2 dl) sugar
 eggs
 teaspoon baking powder
 3/4 cups (350 g) white flour
about 5 1/2 dl)
Decorating: sugar
round cinnamon

. Whip up the eggs and sugar un-
l fluffy and add the eggs one by
ne, beating well.
. Mix the baking powder into the
our and fold into the mixture.
eave the dough to rest in a cool
lace for a couple of hours.
. Shape the dough into short, thin
ticks. Roll in the sugar and cinna-
non mixture and form into
-shapes on the baking tray. Bake
n the oven until golden brown.

Barley cookies
makes about 45)
Preparation time: 1/2 an hour
Resting time for the dough: 2–3
ours
Baking time: about 15 minutes/
batch
Oven temperature: 400 °F (200 °C)
These keep well

1 egg
1/3 cup (100 g) sugar (at least 1 dl)
1/3 cup (100 g) margarine
1 1/2 teaspoons ground cinnamon
1 1/2 cups (about 200 g) barley
flour (4 dl)
1 teaspoon bicarbonate of soda

1. Whip up the egg and sugar.
2. Add the cinnamon, melted margarine and flour and soda mixture.
3. Leave to stand in a cool place
for two or three hours.
4. Roll out into an oblong, about
1/2 cm-thick. Cut out half-moon
shaped biscuits.
5. Bake in the oven until golden
brown.

Rye bread rolls
(makes 50)
Preparation time: about 1 1/2
hours

50 pieces of rye crispbread
3 cups (3/4 l) water
meat extract cube
1/2 lb. (250 g) butter or table
margarine
2 tablespoons mustard
about 1 lb. (400–500 g) grated
sharp cheese

1. Boil up the water and dissolve
the meat extract in it. Grate the
cheese.
2. Dip the crispbread for a moment
in hot meat stock and lay out on
grease-proof paper to soften. Do not
soak them in the stock.
3. Season the softened butter or
table margarine with the mustard
and spread over the soft rye squares.
Cover with grated cheese.
4. Roll up the squares and arrange
on a serving dish with the seams
underneath.
5. Reserve one or two rolls for each
guest. They will keep quite well for
a couple of days.

Feasting in Western Finland

Regional dishes are nowadays very popular for everyday meals and special occasions. Many of them have become regular favourites throughout the country. Others, however, are still only served in specific regions or even individual towns or villages. The dishes traditionally eaten on special occasions in Satakunta, Finland Proper and Häme have many similarities. We have grouped them together under the heading Western Finland. The menu presented here would also be ideally suited for serving at anniversary parties.

Hot and cold buffet
(for 20–30 persons)

Consommé
Pasties
Freshly-salted whitefish (see p. 8)
Rosolli
Salad cream
Veal in aspic
Cheese curds
Garnished chilled fish
Meat balls
Liver and rice casserole
Carrot casserole

Roast veal
Potatoes, carrots and peas
Sweet relish pickle
Prune pudding
Whipped cream

Consommé
Preparation time: 15 minutes
Cooking time: 4 hours
Suitable for freezing

6 lb. (2 1/2 kg) bony beef (shank, breast, oxtail)
16 cups (4 l) water
2 tablespoons salt
15 white peppercorns
2 onions
2 carrots
celerystalks
piece of parsnip
2 bay leaves

1. Rinse the meat and bones thoroughly and place in a large pan. Add the cold water and salt. Bring slowly to the boil and skim off any foam which forms.
2. Add the peppercorns, bay leaves and the scrubbed vegetables.
3. If you want a dark-coloured stock add the onion skins and toast the pieces of vegetable beforehand in a dry, hot frying pan.
4. Simmer for 4–5 hours with the lid tightly on or cook in a pressure cooker for about 1 hour.
5. Strain the stock and remove the layer of fat when cold.
Serve this rich consommé hot with the pasties.
   NOTE: the meat can be minced and used as a filling for the pasties.

Pasties
(makes about 20)
Preparation time: 30 minutes
Baking time: 15 minutes/batch
Oven temperature: 440 °F (225 °C)
Suitable for freezing

Pastry:
One portion of potato pastry (see fish pie, p. 14) or 2 portions of puff pastry (see Christmas star, p. 23) or 1 lb. (500 g) frozen puff pastry.

Arranging this hot and cold buffet for a large number of guests requires much thought and planning. A hand-woven, linen tablecloth makes a fine base. The serving dishes are carefully balanced and the food grouped sensibly around the table. The overall effect is one of peace. The simplicity of the serving dishes shows off the food at its best.

Filling:
1 lb. (500 g) of meat from the con-
sommé or minced beef
1/3 cup (1 dl) cream or sour cream
2 onions
salt to season
a little white pepper

1. Peel and chop up the onions and
fry until transparent.
2. Brown the meat in a frying pan.
3. Add the onion, seasoning and
cream or sour cream and leave to
cool.

4. Roll out the pastry to form a
square about 1 cm thick and cut up
into 8 × 8 cm squares.
5. Fill the center of each square
with the well-seasoned, cold filling.
6. Fold two opposite corners together to form a triangle and seal
the edges. Brush with egg, prick
with a fork and bake in the oven.

Rosolli
Preparation time: 10 minutes + 3
minutes
Cooking time for the vegetables:

30–60 minutes
Not suitable for freezing

7 beets
7 carrots
5 potatoes
2 large dill pickles
2 tart apples
2 onions
salt to taste

1. Boil the vegetables in their skins
the previous day.
2. Peel the vegetables and onions

Chilled fish garnished with plenty of horseradish cream, chives and lemon slices makes an attractive and tasty center-piece.

and cut up finely with a knife or chopper. Do the same with the pickles and apples.

3. Combine the vegetables, onions, pickles, apples and season with salt. Toss with two forks.
Serve the rosolli with salad cream.

Salad cream
Preparation time: 5 minutes

1 3/4 cups (4 dl) cream
2 teaspoons sugar
2 teaspoons vinegar

Whip the cream until thick, add the sugar and vinegar and enough of the beet liquid to give a beautiful pink colour. Serve the salad cream in a separate bowl.

Veal in aspic
Preparation time: 15 minutes + 30 minutes
Cooking time: about 1 hour
Setting time: 1 day
Not suitable for freezing

4 1/2 lb. (2 kg) bony breast or shank of veal
6 cups (1 1/2 l) water
1 tablespoon salt
8 white peppercorns
2 bay leaves
1 onion
1 carrot
3 envelopes Knox gelatin
3 eggs for decorating

1. Rinse the meat, cut up and put in hot water to boil. Skim off any foam and add the sliced onion and carrot and seasoning.
2. Boil the meat until tender. The meat is done when it feels soft and easily separates from the bones.
3. Remove the bones and cut up the meat into small cubes.
4. Strain the stock and cool. Remove the layer of fat from the surface. Dissolve the gelatin in 1/3 cup (1 dl) boiling meat stock. Add

the rest of the stock and check the seasoning.
5. Put the meat in a suitably-shaped dish (breadloaf pan), pour over the gelatin stock and place in a cool place to set.
6. Invert the next day onto a serving dish and garnish with slices of hard-boiled egg.

Cheese curds
Preparation time: 60 minutes
Not suitable for freezing

16 cups (4 l) milk
2 teaspoons rennet
2 teaspoons salt

1. Warm up the milk to lukewarm. Add the rennet and salt and leave in a warm place to curdle for about half an hour.
2. Make incisions down through the curds to the bottom of the pan to let the whey separate completely from the curds.
3. Pour the curds into a cheese mold lined with cheesecloth and press down. Leave to cool in the mold and then invert onto a serving dish.

Hint
Cheese curd made from goats milk is also very tasty.

Garnished chilled fish
Preparation time: 30 minutes
Cooking time: 40 minutes
Cooling time: 1 day
Not suitable for freezing

3 1/2 lb. (1 1/2 kg) whitefish, pike perch or northern pike
4 cups water
1 1/2 tablespoons salt
12 white peppercorns
2 onions
1 bay leaf
a few dill stalks
1 lemon
Horseradish sauce: 1 1/2 cups (4 dl) whipping cream
2 tablespoons sugar
1 tablespoon vinegar
3–4 tablespoons grated horseradish
Garnishing: dill, chives
lemon

1. Clean the fish but do not remove the scales.
2. Place the fish, belly down, in a large pan and cook in well-seasoned stock the day before serving. Simmer on a very low heat. The fish is done when the fins come loose when pulled gently. Cool in the cooking liquid.
3. Remove the skin and place on a serving dish.
4. Whip up the cream and add the sugar, vinegar and grated horseradish. Cover the fish with the horseradish sauce and garnish with dill, chives and slices of lemon.

Meat balls
Preparation time: 30 minutes
Cooking time: 7 minutes/panfull
Suitable for freezing

2 1/4 lb. (1 kg) ground beef
3/4 cups (2 dl) cream
3/4 cups (2 dl) water
1/2 cup (1 1/2 dl) dried bread-crumbs
2 large onions
1 egg
1 tablespoon salt
ground black pepper
oil and butter for frying

1. Stir the breadcrumbs into the water and cream mixture.
2. Finely chop the onions and fry until golden brown.
3. Mix together the minced beef, spices, onions, egg and breadcrumb mixture.
4. Mix well together. Rub the palms of your hands with a little oil and form small balls of the mixture. The oil will prevent splattering and stop the meat balls from losing their color if they are left to stand before frying.

Liver and rice casserole
Preparation time: 30 minutes
Cooking time: 20 minutes + 1 1/2–2 hours
Oven temperature: 350 °F (175 °C)
Suitable for freezing

3/4 cups (2 dl) rice
1 1/2 cups (4 dl) water
1/2 cup (1,2 dl) milk
3 teaspoons salt

2 medium-sized onions
1/4 cup (50 g) butter
1/3–3/4 cup (1–2 dl) raisins
4 tablespoons dark Karo syrup
1 teaspoon white pepper
1 teaspoon marjoram
1 egg
1 1/4 cups (300 g) minced calf's
liver or beef's liver

1. Boil the rice in the water and milk mixture and cook until the rice starts to thicken just a bit.
2. Peel and chop the onions and sauté in a little butter.
3. Mix the liver, chopped onion, raisins, seasoning and egg into the cooled-down rice pudding. The mixture should be rather loose.
4. Pour into a greased baking dish and dot with butter. Bake in a medium oven until golden brown on top. Serve with melted butter and lingonberry preserves.

Hint
Whole pearl barley, which has been soaked overnight in cold water, can be used instead of rice.

Carrot casserole
Preparation time: 40 minutes
Cooking time: 20 minutes + 1 1/2–2 hours
Oven temperature: 350 °F (175 °C)
Suitable for freezing

3/4 cup (2 dl) rice
1 1/2 cups (4 dl) water
1/2 cup (1,2 dl) milk
3 teaspoons salt
3 lb. (1 1/2 kg) carrots
3/4 cup (2 dl) milk or a mixture of cream and milk
1/4 cup (50 g) butter
3 eggs
1 teaspoon grated nutmeg
1 tablespoon sugar
2 teaspoons salt
Coating: dried breadcrumbs
butter

Prune pudding topped with whipped cream is a dessert traditionally served in Western Finland.

1. Cook the rice as for the previous recipe.
2. Peel and grate the carrots.
3. Mix the grated carrots, milk, melted butter, eggs and spices into the rice pudding.
4. Pour the mixture into a greased baking dish. Sprinkle with dried breadcrumbs and dot with butter.
Bake in the oven until brown all over.

Roast veal
Preparation time: 10 minutes
Roasting time: 3 hours
Oven temperature: 300 °F (150 °C)
Suitable for freezing

5–6 lb. (2 1/2 kg) veal roast
1 tablespoon salt
2 onions
2 carrots
Gravy: 1 1/2–2 cups (4–5 dl) juices from the roast
3–4 tablespoons white flour
3/4 cup (2 dl) cream

1. Place the roast on a wire rack in a roasting pan and put in the oven.
2. Put the cleaned carrots and onions in a roasting pan. Rub salt over the joint after it is browned.
3. Roast in the oven until the roasting thermometer reads about 170 °F (77 °C). Pour some water into the roasting pan to prevent the juices from burning.
4. Prepare the gravy by thickening the meat juices with the flour. Boil for 10 minutes, add the cream and check the seasoning.
Serve with boiled potatoes, carrots, peas and tangy relish pickle.

Hint
The gravy can also be prepared by making a pureé from the cooked carrots and onions

Prune pudding
Preparation time: 5 minutes
Soaking time: overnight
Cooking time: 20 minutes

6 cups (1 1/2 l) water
1 lb. (1/2 kg) dried prunes
1 stick of cinnamon
1/2 cup (1 1/2 dl) sugar
5 tablespoons potato starch

Topping: 1 1/4 cups (3 dl) cream
2 tablespoons sugar

1. Soak the prunes in cold water overnight.
2. Add the sugar and cinnamon stick to the soaking liquid and cook until the prunes are soft. Thicken with potato starch mixed in a little cold water (see stewed rhubarb, p. 9). Pour into dessert bowls and sprinkle with a little sugar. NOTE: if the bowls are made of glass, put a metal spoon in first to stop the glass cracking. Cool in room temperature.
3. Top when cold with sweetened whipped cream.

Hint
Stewed prune pudding
Preparation time: 10 minutes
Soaking time: overnight
Cooking time: 20 minutes
Setting time: 2–3 hours

1 cup (250 g) dried prunes
2 cups (5 dl) water
1/3 cup (1 dl) sugar
2 cups (5 dl) cream
3 envelopes Knox gelatin

1. Soak the prunes overnight in 1 3/4 cups (4 dl) cold water.
2. Cook the prunes in the soaking liquid with the sugar until soft. Mash the prunes with a fork or whisk.
3. Whip up the cream.
4. Dissolve the gelatin in 1/3 cup (1 dl) boiling water.
5. Combine the mashed prunes with the gelatin and, when it has cooled a little, mix in the whipped cream. Pour into a serving bowl and leave to set.

Feasting in Lapland

Braised reindeer and salmon soup are real delicies of Lapland. The braised reindeer is enjoyed by lapps as well as their foreign guests.

This dish is easily and quickly prepared, just as it has always been done by the reindeer herdsmen on cold winter days around a campfire.

Company fare
(for 10 persons)

Finnish salmon soup
Unleavened barley bread

Braised reindeer
Mashed potatoes
Cranberries or lingonberries
Homemade beer

Homemade flat cheese

Coffee

Finnish salmon soup
Preparation time: 40 minutes
Cooking time: 30 minutes
Not suitable for freezing

3 lb. (1 1/2 kg) salmon or rainbow trout
10 cups (2 1/2 l) water
1–2 tablespoons salt
1 onion
5 white peppercorns
4 cups (1 l) peeled, cubed potatoes
1/2 cup (100 g) butter
fresh dill

1. Clean the fish and cut up into portions.
2. Boil the salt and finely-chopped onion in a saucepan. Add the cooked potatoes, portions of fish, peppercorns and butter. Cook over a medium heat for half an hour. Add chopped dill to the stew when ready and check the seasoning.

Hint
If you want to make this stew without any fish bones in it, fillet the fish and make a fish stock from the head and backbone. Prepare the stew from the strained stock.

Unleavened barley bread
(makes 3–4 loaves)
Preparation time: 15 minutes
Baking time: 10–15 minutes
Oven temperature: 575 °F (300 °C)
Not suitable for freezing

2 cups (1 1/2 l) cold water or milk
(1/2 tablespoon yeast)
1 tablespoon salt
2 1/4 lbs. (about 1 kg) barley flour

1. Add salt (and yeast) to the cold liquid and make into dough with the barley flour.
2. Divide the dough up into 3–4 large portions. Shape the dough into large balls and then roll out or pat into flat, thin, circular loaves. (Prick all over with a fork.)
3. Bake the loaves in the oven or on a griddle. Place the loaves on top of each other when done and cover with a clean cloth. Serve the bread warm.

Hint
A mixture of water and sour milk can also be used, but in this case one teaspoon of bicarbonate of soda should be added to the flour.

Braised reindeer
Preparation time: 10 minutes
Cooking time: 30 minutes
Suitable for freezing

3 lb. (1 1/2 kg) frozen reindeer meat or venison
3/4–1 lb. (300–400 g) freshside of pork or bacon
1 tablespoon salt
10 whole allspice
1 1/4 cup (3 dl) water

A blazing log fire and a wall hanging "Raanu" make a vivid setting for the meal. Salmon soup and braised reindeer are brought piping hot to the table without having to change dishes. Coffee is served in good-sized mugs, leaving plenty of room for home-made flat cheese to be crumbled in.

1. Cut up the pork or bacon into thin strips and brown in a cooking pot. Cut the frozen reindeer meat into thin strips, add in small amounts to the pot and brown.
2. Add the seasoning and the water. Cook slowly with the lid on until done.

Butter or oil can also be used instead of the pork or bacon.

Mashed potatoes
Preparation time: 15 minutes
Cooking time: 30 minutes
Not suitable for freezing

4 1/2 lb. (2 kg) potatoes
water
salt to taste
2 3/4 cups (6–7 dl) milk or, instead of the milk,
1/2 cups (1 1/2 dl) powdered milk and
2 3/4 cups (7 dl) of the potato water
1 tablespoon salt
1 tablespoon butter

1. Peel the potatoes and place in slightly-salted boiling water.
2. When the potatoes are cooked, drain but retain the water if you are going to use powdered milk. Mash the potatoes with a hand masher or electric mixer. Add the hot milk or powdered milk and potato water.
3. Beat the mixture until light, add the salt and butter and check the seasoning.

Homemade beer
Preparation time: 10 minutes + 10 minutes
Fermentation time: 2–3 days

1 1/2 cups (4 dl) malt flour
3/4 cup (2 dl) sugar
1/2–1 teaspoon yeast
24 cups (6 l) water

1. Heat up the water and pour over the sugar and malt. Cool down the liquid to hand temperature and add the yeast dissolved in a little water.
2. Leave to ferment for one day at room temperature, strain and then bottle. Keep the bottles in a cool place.

Homemade flat cheese
Preparation time: 1 hour
Baking time: 10–15 minutes
Oven temperature: 575 °F (300 °C)
Suitable for freezing

24 cups (6 l) milk
1 tablespoon rennet
2 teaspoons salt

1. Mix the rennet and salt in the lukewarm milk. Leave to curdle in a warm place (see cheese curds, p. 55) and separate out the curds with a sieve.
2. Form the curds into a round cake, about 2 cm thick, and place on a cookie sheet.
3. Bake the cheese in a hot oven or under a grill until the surface is dotted with brown patches.

NOTE: the proper way to eat this cheese is to crumble it into pieces and add to hot coffee.

Feasting in Karelia

*»Ask the guest to sit
and rest him.
With the guest converse
in friendship,
With thy talk amuse
the stranger,
till the dinner shall be ready»*
(Kalevala)

*We have inherited a rich
culinary tradition from
Karelia — the land of song.
We have chosen only a few
of the most typical Karelian
dishes here, which even a
beginner will be able to
make.*

Come and get it!
(for 10 persons)

*Karelian rice pasties
Salted fish
Mushroom salad*

*Karelian potato pasties
Karelian ragoût
Dill pickles*

Lingonberry pudding

In addition to Karelian rice pasties,
salted fish can also be served as an
appetizer: salted vendace or freshly-
salted whitefish (see p. 8). Wild
mushrooms prepared in many different ways form an integral part of
Karelian cuisine.

Karelian rice pasties
(makes 20)
Preparation time: 1 hour
Baking time: 5–7 minutes/batch
Oven temperature: 575 °F (300 °C)
Suitable for freezing

*Lingonberries are the most versa-
tile of the berries found growing in
the forests in Finland. Here they
provide a refreshing dessert.*

*Pastry: 3/4 cup (2 dl) water
1 1/2 teaspoons salt
1 1/4 cups (3 dl) rye flour
3/4 cup (2 dl) white flour
Filling: (20 pasties):
1/2 portion of rice pudding (see
p. 16) or
1/2 portion of mashed potatoes (see
p. 60)
1 egg
3/4 cup (2 dl) boiling milk and
3 tablespoons butter for brushing
the pasties*

1. Prepare the filling and mix in
one egg.

2. Mix together the water, salt and
flour.

3. Shape the dough into a long
rope the thickness of your wrist and
cut into 20 equal portions. Shape
the pieces into round flat cakes and
form into a pile at the side of the
baking table. Roll out each cake
into a very thin circle. Set aside,
but not on top of each other as they
will stick together.

4. Fill the center of each with the
rice pudding or mashed potatoes,
fold over the edges and pinch
tightly.

5. Bake for a short time in a hot

oven. Brush the pasties when done with the milk and butter mixture and leave to soften in a dish under a cloth.

Karelian ragoût
Preparation time: 20 minutes
Cooking time: 4–5 hours
Oven temperature: 300 °F (150 °C)
Suitable for freezing

1 lb. (500 g) pork
1 lb. (500 g) mutton
1 lb. (500 g) beef
water
1 1/2 tablespoon salt
2 onions
15–20 whole allspice

1. Cut up the meat into chunks and place in a casserole dish.
2. Add the salt, allspice and onions and pour over enough boiling water to just cover the meat.
3. Cook in a slow oven until tender. Cover the dish with a lid towards the end of the cooking time.

Lingonberry pudding
Preparation time: 20 minutes
Cooking time: 5 minutes

6 cups (1 1/2 l) water
1/3 cup 1 dl) sugar
7–8 tablespoons potato starch
2 cups (1/2 l) lingonberries or lingonberry or cranberry preserves

1. Mix together the water, sugar and potato starch in a saucepan. Bring slowly to the boil stirring continuously.
2. Add the mashed lingonberries when the mixture has cooled a little. Pour into dessert bowls and sprinkle with sugar to prevent a skin forming on top.

The table is dominated by the colors of Karelia — red and black. They are repeated in the table cloth, in the serving dishes, even in the lingonberry pudding which is served in individual bowls. The whole arrangement is set off with a spring of juniper in a wooden bowl.

Index

Table Settings

Midsummer
Tablecloth *Ilma*, Tampella
Dishes *Arctica*, *Kokki*, Arabia
Glasses *Laguuni*, *Elegia*, Nuutajärvi Glass
Cutlery *Carelia*, Hackman
Garden Party in the Summer
Tablecloth *Napakka*, Marimekko
Dishes *Kesti*, *Uunikokki*, Arabia
Glasses *Luna*, Nuutajärvi Glass
Kettle, coffee pot *Finella*, Järvenpää Enamel
Cutlery *Savonia*, Hackman
Autumn Fish Festival
Dishes *Kokki*, Arabia
Glasses *Virva*, *Luna*, Nuutajärvi Glass
Cutlery *Tumppi*, Hackman
Christmas Porridge on Christmas Eve
Dishes *Ruska*, Arabia
Cutlery *Lion*, Hackman

Traditional Christmas Eve Dinner
Tablecloth *Poppana*, Oiliina
Dishes *Ruska*, Arabia
Glasses *Luna*, *Laguuni*, *Hiiop*, Nuutajärvi Glass
Cutlery *Carelia*, Hackman
Grandma's Christmas Coffee Table
Dishes *Myrna*, Arabia
Glasses *Apila*, Nuutajärvi Glass
Boxing Day
Tablecloth *Pastilli*, Marimekko
Dishes *Pudas*, Arabia
Glasses *Arctica*, *Filigraani*, Nuutajärvi Glass
New Year's Eve
Tablecloth *Tanhu*, Metsovaara
Dishes *Teema*, *Kasino*, Arabia
Casserole dishes *Riistapata*, Järvenpää Enamel
Mugs, Järvenpää Enamel
Bowl *Virva*, Nuutajärvi Glass
Cutlery *Carelia*, Hackman
Lenten Supper
Tablecloth *Hand-woven*
Dishes *Kasino*, *Kokki*, Arabia
Cutlery *Savonia*, Hackman
Easter Dinner
Tablecloth, Friends of Finnish Handicraft
Dishes *Teema*, Arabia
Glasses *Irish coffee*, *Luna*, Nuutajärvi Glass
Cutlery *Tumppi*, Hackman
Christening Party
Tablecloth, Metsovaara
Dishes *Arctica*, Arabia
Cake dish *Filigraani*, Nuutajärvi Glass
Children's Birthday Parties
Glasses *Luna*, *Irish coffee*, Nuutajärvi Glass
Mugs, Järvenpää Enamel
Graduation Party
Tablecloth *Satiini*, Metsovaara
Dishes *Valencia*, Arabia
Glasses *Herttua*, *Laguuni*, Nuutajärvi Glass
House-warming Party
Tablecloth *Riite*, Marimekko
Dishes *Salla*, Arabia
Glass bowl *Laguuni*, Nuutajärvi Glass
Anniversaries
Tablecloth *Pellavankukka*, Vuorelma
Dishes *Seita*, Arabia
Cutlery *Tapio*, and silver service, Kultakeskus
Feasting in Western Finland
Tablecloth, Friends of Finnish Handicraft
Dishes *Teema*, Arabia
Glasses *Herttua*, Nuutajärvi Glass
Cutlery *Savonia*, Hackman
Feasting in Lapland
Tablecloth, Metsovaara
Dishes *Karelia*, Arabia
Glasses *Luna*, Nuutajärvi Glass
Kettles *Finella*, *Rautarouva*, Järvenpää Enamel
Cutlery *Savonia*, Hackman
Feasting in Karelia
Tablecloth *Pellava*, Vokki-Virkki
Dishes *Teema*, Arabia
Glasses *Luna*, Nuutajärvi Glass
Casserole dish *Nurmesniemi*, Järvenpää Enamel
Cutlery *Carelia*, Hackman